THE PROBLEM OF
DOING YOUR OWN THING

THE PROBLEM OF DOING YOUR OWN THING

BOB MUMFORD

BOB mumford

Box 22341 • Ft. Lauderdale, Florida 33315 • (305) 524-3349

This book is appearing serially in New Wine Magazine, © copyright 1972, 1973, published by Christian Growth Ministries, Fort Lauderdale, Florida.

ISBN 0-8007-8129-5

CONTENTS

INTRODUCTION

Zephaniah described his day, and prophetically, described ours when he said:

> "She obeyed not the voice; she received not correction; she trusted not in the Lord; she drew not near to her God." Zephaniah 3:2.

Anyone who has tried to walk with God has faced the universal problem of "doing his own thing" — that innate nature of rebellion and disobedience in the face of God's authority. The Church — each one of us individually — must find the way of *release* — the *solution* to this most common of spiritual dilemmas.

The following six chapters are an earnest effort to provide that solution by defining the problem as we meet it in daily life and making clear the difference between the *desire* to obey and the *ability* to obey.

These chapters were taken from a recorded series of teachings entitled *The Spirit and Nature of Obedience* written initially for publication in New Wine Magazine. They are now set forth in book form with the earnest desire that its message will be heard — and in hearing yield the peaceable fruit of the Spirit!

The book *Spiritual Authority,* by Watchman Nee, crystallized many of these concepts for me and gave me the encouragement needed to speak out on this critical theme.

God, our Father, may the Lordship of Jesus be revealed through these pages in such a manner as to save us from doing our own thing. Amen.

Bob Mumford

NOTE: The seven recorded messages entitled *The Nature and Spirit of Obedience,* are available on reel or cassette from: P.O. Box 22341, Fort Lauderdale, Florida 33315.

Chapter One

THE SPIRIT OF LAWLESSNESS

"Lawlessness" means different things to different people. Some instantly hear the shrill of a siren, the screech of tires sliding to a halt, and the clank of hand-cuffs. Another will be caught up in the suspense of a courtroom scene with judge poised to pronounce the sentence; the accused, belligerent, in the face of the verdict. Still another may only be conscious of his own inner burning resentment and the discipline necessary to keep it from erupting into action. But how many picture a Christian standing accused, amazed and questioning, at the discovery of his own lawlessness before the Word of God?

Certain principles are present in every instance of lawlessness. It is these basic principles that we are probing in our search toward understanding the Nature and Spirit of Obedience. Lawlessness and obedience are two sides of the same coin. Man has been endowed with the privilege of choosing which side of the coin he will use in the daily exchange of life.

Personally, I have been working on this word "lawlessness" for six or seven years. There is within my heart a cry to understand obedience in some new way — some deeper way than I have ever known it before. Everyone who has dealt with the things of God for very long knows that an individual shares out of his own needs. A true teaching results from the search of a man who has been crying out for understanding.

For an introduction to the character of lawlessness, we take three verses from the closing of Jesus' teaching which is often referred to as The Beatitudes — Matthew 7:21—23:

"Not every one that saith unto me, Lord, Lord shall enter into the kingdom of heaven; but he that doeth the will of my father which is in heaven. Many will say to me in that day, Lord, Lord, have we not prophesied in thy name? and in thy name have cast out devils: and in thy name done many wonderful works (i.e., miracles, healings, other signs and wonders). *And then will I profess unto them, I never knew you: depart from me, ye that work iniquity."*

Notice that the party in question calls Jesus "Lord". I Corinthians 12:3 tells us, ". . . no man can say that Jesus is the Lord, but by the Holy Ghost." It is my belief that these three verses refer to born-again, Spirit-filled Christians.

Consider the phrase, "Not every one that saith unto me, Lord, Lord, shall enter into the kingdom of heaven." As I understand it, this does not mean heaven in the ultimate sense, but refers to relationships and involvements in this present life, as well as to the future.

In the following phrase, ". . . but he that doeth the *will* of my Father which is in heaven . . .", the word *will* could be translated the *desire* or the *wish* of my Father. In most instances it is translated this way. It is the same word that is used by Jesus (Matthew 6:10) when He teaches us to pray, ". . . Thy *will* be done in earth, as it is in heaven." It is the desire, or the wish, of the very heartbeat of God which is expressed in this word *will.*

So Jesus is saying, "Not everyone who says to me Lord, Lord, shall enter into the kingdom of heaven, but he that does the wish, the desire, the will of my Father which is in heaven. Many will say to me in that day, Lord, Lord, have we not prophesied in thy name . . ."

Here let us consider three verses from the Book of Mark — 9:38—40. "And John answered him, saying, Master, we saw one casting out devils in thy name and he followed not us: and we forbad him, because he followeth us not. But Jesus said, Forbid him not: for there is no man which shall do a miracle in my name, that can lightly speak evil of me. For he that is not against us is on our part."

Looking again at Matthew 7:22, ". . . have we not prophesied in thy name? and in thy name have cast out demons? and in thy name have done many wonderful works? And then will I profess unto them, I have never *approved* (many translations use this word and the Greek substantiates it) you. Depart from me, ye that work *iniquity.*"

Here is the word I have been after — INIQUITY! Immediately there leaps into the mind of most Christians visions of robbing banks, beating up your grandmother, and all sorts of lurid crimes. We think, "Oh, those nasty people, no wonder the Lord says I never knew you." But the interesting thing is, the Lord does know them. So there must be something further as far as interpreting what Jesus means when He said, "I never knew you." He cannot be saying, "I don't know your name or address." What is He saying, then? In this instance, iniquity is *lawlessness.*

That is, they were walking without law. Please let me say right here as strongly as I know how — much of the Christian community is walking without law!

DOING YOUR OWN THING

Which brings up this question. Is it possible to know and understand the things of the Spirit, grab them to ourselves and go our own ways? The answer is a resounding YES!

One important principle which we need to realize is this: the ultimate law in all the Universe is the will of God. There is no law above the will of God.

How about a Mumford translation of our three verses from Matthew: "They called Him Lord because they loved Him. But He says: Why do you call Me Lord when you don't want to do the things that I tell you? If you are going to call Me Lord, then you must come under a spirit of obedience. You see, it's not what needs to be done. It's what I tell you to do. But you call me Lord, Lord, and you take the things of the Spirit and you use them to your own promotion, to do your own thing, to go your own way and build 'something for Jesus'."

Do you know that it is not what you do, and it is not where you go; but it is whether or not you have done the will of God?

I may say to God, "God, I am going to Philadelphia and preach the gospel." He replies, "You stay in Fort Lauderdale!"

"But God, I want to go to Philadelphia and I enjoy preaching and I am going to save the world for Jesus! Move over, God!"

Or, we may become acutely aware of a need on the

other side of the world. So off we go — without background, training, commission — simply because there is a need. There is only one thing wrong with the whole set-up: it wasn't within the revealed will of the Lord for you!

These instances remind me of the time I rode a horse on a dare. It was a big white mare and the moment I got on the horse she became aware that I did not know how to ride. So the horse took the bit in her teeth and dashed off just where she wanted to go. I didn't have a thing to say about it! I just rode along. This is the way it can happen with the things of the Spirit. We get the bit in our teeth and dash off to do something for Jesus, and the Lord just rides along, waiting for the day when He can get the bit into our mouths and get us stopped long enough to direct us into whatever He wanted us to do in the first place.

Do you see it? I take the things of God and go my own way. Therefore, He says, "If you do that, you will find out that you are going to be disapproved. This is not what I am after in your life. I cannot use you. I find that I must reject you, not as a child of God, but I must reject you because of your *lawlessness* — because you refuse to come under law."

Now, Church, the strange part of this whole thing is that nobody has trouble "obeying" until God's will crosses his will! Also, how many of us have found out that God knows just where to place His finger in order to reveal to us our lawlessness?

This has nothing to do with open sin. It has to do with the inward nature of obedience. *Lawlessness is a spirit.* It is something within the child of God that we received from our father Adam that came right down to us. When God's will crosses our will — that is when we discover the spirit within us that responds, "But I want to do my own thing!" We super-impose our own will on God's will . . . *and this is lawlessness.*

An example of this truth of lawlessness and disapproval is in Ezekiel 44:10—15. "And the Levites (notice, these were men of God) that are gone away far from me, when Israel went astray, which went astray away from me after their idols: (doing their own thing) they shall bear their *iniquity.* (Here is the same word — *lawlessness.)*

Yet they shall be ministers in my sanctuary, having charge at the gates of the house, and ministering to the house; they shall slay the burnt offering and the sacrifice for the people, and they shall stand before them to minister to them."

The verses which follow do not say, "Those Levites that went after their idols — I am going to cut them off and have nothing more to do with them." No, this is what God says, "This is a *lawless spirit,* and because of this comes rejection and a certain punishment. You priests may continue to stand before the people and minister to them, but you may not come near to me anymore — nor to any of my holy things; only those who did not go astray can stand before me."

I believe this is almost an ultimate punishment — "you go ahead and minister but what I am after is sons of righteousness . . . those who obey . . . those who want to do My will . . . where there is a spirit inside the man which says, 'I delight to do Thy will, O God'."

Yes, you can take the things of God and go build

your own church . . . your own prayer
group . . . your own doctrine. The worst part of it is
that God blesses it. But the lawless spirit within you
will ultimately call forth rejection and punishment.

If I could blow an urgent trumpet, the message
would be: for Jesus' sake, seek to hear and
understand what God is saying to us in this area!
Each one of us will have to discover for himself his
own spirit of *lawlessness*. Because we have thrown off
outward sin, we have difficulty recognizing that the
spirit of rebellion, the spirit of anarchy, is at work in
our lives. What God is really after is to write *His* law
on our hearts.

GOD'S REVEALED WILL

Psalm 19 has much to teach us along these lines. It
shows us the three ways by which God makes Himself
known to man: general revelation; special revelation;
and spiritual revelation, where God makes Himself
known through the Spirit in the inner man.

Verses 1–6 gives us a general revelation:

*"The heavens declare the glory of God; and the
firmament sheweth His handiwork.*

*"Day unto day uttereth speech, and night unto
night, sheweth knowledge.*

*"There is no speech nor language, where their voice
is not heard.*

*"Their line is gone out through all the earth, and
their words to the end of the world. In them hath he
set a tabernacle for the sun.*

*"Which is as a bridegroom coming out of his
chambers and rejoiceth as a strong man to run a race.*

"His going forth is from the end of the heaven, and

his circuit unto the ends of it, and there is nothing hid from the heat thereof."

Pictured for us is a man looking upward. He sees the heavens spread before him. He sees the light . . . the dark . . . the stars. To many, these glories proclaim the Creatorship of God. To others the scene leaves only questions with no answers.

One day a professor was talking with a student who claimed to be an agnostic. The student said, "I want to know God and yet I don't believe there is any God."

To which the professor replied, "Go out in the back yard and lift your head up and say, 'God, if there is a God, I want to know you.' "

After following these suggestions the boy returned and his professor asked, "How did you make out?"

The response was, "I felt like a fool."

"Good!" came the answer, "That's the way to start."

Here we see the workings of general revelation. However, there is no voice, there is no speech. This can be very dangerous because people will say, "Yes, God is a creator. I believe in God. I see His handiwork." The result of such limited acceptance ends in pantheism and religion. It is dangerous because people get excited and feel they believe in God just because they see evidence of His creative powers. Even the devils believe in God.

Yes, general revelation is a step in the right direction, but it falls very short of God's desired goal to make Himself known to man. General revelation can tell you that He is, but it can never tell you what His will is for you. God wants to be known, but He also wants you to know what He is like. He said, "If you want to know what I am like, then read about it."

Verses 7—10 contain a special revelation of God:

"The law of the Lord is perfect, converting the soul; the testimony of the Lord is sure making wise the simple.

"The statutes of the Lord are right, rejoicing the heart; the commandment of the Lord is pure, enlightening the eyes.

"The fear of the Lord is clean, enduring forever; the judgments of the Lord are true and righteous altogether.

"More to be desired are they than gold, yea, than much fine gold; sweeter also than honey and the honeycomb.

"Moreover by them is thy servant warned; and in keeping of them there is great reward."

Yes, once we see God in creation, He has what is called Special Revelation for us. Many, or perhaps most, of us have mental images of God. These are the products of our imaginations of what God is like. And He may not be at all like that! God provided for that possibility. He said, as we have mentioned before, "If you want to know what I am like, *read* about it."

Special Revelation tells us just this and much more. It shows us His provisions for all of our needs and in this we get a picture of His greatness . . . His goodness . . . His wisdom.   These are insights we never could receive through just General Revelation. He also tells us what He wants us to do . . . where to go . . . what to say . . . how to dress . . . what He expects from us. This is God dealing with the individual. His ultimate goal is, that after years of rebellion, each one may have revealed to him the specific will of God in every detail of his life.

Finally, we see a spiritual revelation of God in verses 12–14:

"Who can understand his errors? cleanse thou me from secret faults.

"Keep back thy servant also from presumptuous sins; let them not have dominion over me: then shall I be upright, and I shall be innocent from the great transgression.

"Let the words of my mouth and the meditations of my heart be acceptable in thy sight,

"O, Lord, my strength and my redeemer."

Spiritual Revelation occurs when God *works* what He is and what He reveals Himself to be, into the heart of man.

Jeremiah, Ezekiel and the Book of Hebrews all teach us that God's ultimate goal is to open us up and write His laws on our hearts. Jeremiah says, "I will give him a new heart." Ezekiel puts it this way, "I will sprinkle you and write my laws on your heart." In Hebrews chapters 8 and 10, we find: "I write my laws on your heart."

The motion picture, THE TEN COMMANDMENTS, portrayed for us the scene of God's laws being engraved upon the tablets of stone. As I witnessed this, I saw what God's ultimate intention was and what He wants to do *within* us. When His law is written on the table of a person's heart, there will not be a *lawless* spirit, but a spirit eager to do His will.

One translation of the question asked in this Spiritual Revelation as "Who can understand his errors?", words it this way, "Who can tell how many times we offend?" This is a question David is asking, "Who can understand how many times we must have offended God and walked off in a lawless spirit, without even knowing it?"

David closes the Psalm with the prayer, "Let the words of my mouth . . ." Do you realize the truth implied in this opening phrase? Another reminder from scripture says, "Out of the heart the mouth speaks." It really is true. The meditations of the heart are expressed through the mouth. In Spiritual Revelation the Word is made flesh.

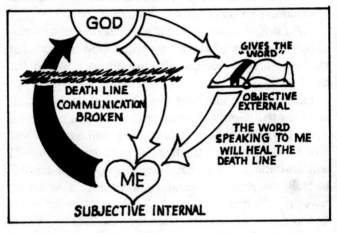

GOD'S PLAN FOR MAN

In order to explain how God works in the life of man, let me use the above illustration and then take myself as an example. I know myself better than I know anyone else and I know His workings in my life.

There is one thing that I want in life — I want to know Him. My heart beats inside. It beats out a desire and says, "God, I want to know You. I want to

understand You. I want to come to love You and be a
son who is pleasing to You." This is all working in my
heart and I say, "God, reveal Yourself to me."

But something happened to impede the fulfillment
of these desires. Sin entered in and caused what we
shall call the *death line*. In the rupture, the
communication between God and me was cut off.
Due to this death line, my spirit, and all that was
involved, died. We are all familiar with this alienation
between God and man.

But God said, "Mumford, I still love you."

Amazed, I responded, "You do?"

"Yes," He answered, "and in order for Me to reveal
My love to you I have to give you something – the
written Word. This will speak to you and if you will
permit it to, we can get this death line healed."

You will notice in our drawing showing the
communication lines between God and me, that His
plan is *double arrows*. It is not just me going to God,
but it is God coming to me. This is extremely
important! In fact, this is where we are most apt to
ruin the entire procedure.

The minute the death line is healed, we are apt to
think we know God, not literally but actually. We fail
to remember that this is a progressive revealing of
God's will.

Right here we are going to take two words. The
first is *SUBJECTIVE* or *INTERNAL*. The second is
OBJECTIVE or *EXTERNAL*. The first is what is going
on inside of me. The other is what is going on outside
of me. The external, or objective, is what the
scripture calls *TRUTH*. The embodiment of Truth is
God's *LAW*. Jesus said, "Thy word is truth". (John
17:17). Here is God's inspired Word given to us (special

revelation) to tell us what He is like, what He wants from us, what He expects us to do. It includes our money, how we are to handle our sex life, when and where He wants us to go to church. This is called the perspicuity of scripture — meaning that the Bible speaks to everything. If you do not believe that it does — just read it!

To single out one experience which proves this, let me tell you about my purchase of a Christmas tree. The price was $5.00 and I felt this was more than I wanted to pay. So I began haggling with the merchant. I said, "That little thing! It is half dead already. Look, the limbs are beginning to fall off."

"Well, I'll give it to you for $3.50," said the salesman. I gave him the money and got in the car.

I drove home thinking, "Boy, did I get a bargain!" That night before I got in bed, I picked up my Bible and a verse in Proverbs (20:14) jumped out at me. "It is worthless, it is worthless, says the buyer; but when he goes his way, then he boasts (about his bargain)." (Amplified).

Convicted, I cried, "God, you got me! This is exactly what I did." Recalling how I tried to get the salesman to come down on his price and how he finally agreed to sell the tree for $3.50, I realized I had sold myself for $1.50. Big deal! But I did not know. Do you know why I did not know? Subjectively, I think I know things. Internally, I am Lord in my house . . . I have to make my own decisions and go my own way. God said, "I know that, but I'll tell you what I have done, son. I have given to you something *outside* of yourself that will show you how to do this."

The Father is *searching* for a people who will

worship Him in spirit and truth. Jesus made it very plain when He said, "The Father seeks such to worship Him in spirit and truth." (John 4:23). He has given to us His Spirit and His Truth. Together they lead to spiritual health and growth. Someone has said, "The Word alone, you dry up; the Spirit alone, you blow up; the Spirit and Truth, you grow up."

F.B. Meyer tells a story about going to visit an older man who loved God with all of his heart. One morning about 5:30 o'clock Mr. Meyer came up the stairs into the friend's room to find him pouring over the scriptures. He asked, "What are you doing?"

The reply was, "Well, I am just finding out whether I love the Lord or not."

Surprise was evident in the next question, "You find out whether or not you love the Lord?"

"Yes," the old man replied, "I read the verse that says, 'He that has my commandments and keeps them, he it is that loves me.' I have just been going over the commandments to find out whether or not I really love Him."

Perhaps we had better ask ourselves if it is possible to come into a religious self-deception and believe that we are something that we really are not. If I ask myself the question, "Do I really love the Lord?", and seek to answer it from merely the way *I feel,* I may be deceiving myself. But if I have a way of measuring my answer, I am obligated to put that method into use.

But how can we measure correctly if we are not acquainted with the *ruler* (the Word of God)? We are going to have to learn that there is a nasty word that is used perhaps a hundred times in the New Testament — that word is *commandments.* We don't even like the thought of that word! We rear back and say, "Are you trying to put me under the law?" You had better believe it — a new kind of law.

If you can see this principle starting to work in your life, you will pour over the scriptures, coming to the place where you will ask yourself, "Am I doing that? Am I obeying this?" It is important that we see this subjective-objective relationship which will lead to spiritual health and keep us walking in the light of God's Word.

SIX GUIDELINES ON THE RULER

Returning to our thoughts on Special Revelation, we find six definite guidelines for measuring our understanding of God's provisions for spiritual growth and maturity. These are progressive. They have been tested, tried and proved over many centuries of use.

"The law of the Lord is perfect, converting the soul." The word "law" is used in many different ways in the scriptures, but here it literally means "to point the finger". It means you are going one way and God says, "Go this way." This is general direction. The *law* of the Lord is perfect, turning you around — sending you in a different way. It is the finger pointing you. It might be called the "over-view" — it is over everything. It shows you how He wants things to be done.

"The testimony of the Lord is sure making wise the simple." Literally translated in both Hebrew and Greek, testimony simply means that "it works!" If you do what the *law* tells you to do, the *testimony* is this — it works! Most of us could give testimony

after testimony about God's ways working. I have never in my life had anyone tell me that God had actually failed him. If you meet God's qualifications, you will find that it always works. It is sure and it makes you wise. It affords an internal knowledge — not an academic wisdom — but an intellectual knowing of that which is real from that which is not.

"The statutes of the Lord are right, rejoicing the heart." This has to do with civil and human relationships. We all know that there are a multitude of crying needs in our world today. And there are almost as many solutions offered as there are problems. But God gives certain *statutes* governing civil, human and inter-personal relationships. If we would live by these *statutes,* we would not have the racial, economic, social snarls with which we are beset. They would be unraveled through the *statutes* given to us for these purposes. The effect would be a rejoicing in the home, the community, the church — such as never has been seen before in the history of the world. Joy leaves when you break God's *statutes.*

"The commandment of the Lord is pure, enlightening the eyes." Commandment means special instruction clearly given. His command is pure, which is better translated clear, plain or distinct. One command given to us by Jesus is, "A new commandment give I unto you, that you love one another." It is plain. He told us to do it. It will open our eyes. When we do what the Lord tells us to do, it is amazing what we see following our obedience. God opens whole new vistas and horizons to the obedient. The disobedient go dry.

"The fear of the Lord is clean, enduring forever."
This is the motivation for holy living — the fear of
the Lord keeps you clean. Someone may say, "It
doesn't mean to be scared of God." Oh yes, it does!
It would be good for all of us who are seeking to
follow the Lord to get a good dose of fear. Don't play
games with Him. He will get you in the end.
Judgment is not always speedily executed but He will
get you. It may take a year, or five, or twenty years,
but He will be there waiting for you. The fear of the
Lord keeps you clean.

For example . . . the eyes of the Lord are
watching when you make out your income tax. When
you know He is going to be watching, it is strange
how easy it is to put in the right figures! Uncle Sam
may be on the alert occasionally, but the judgment of
the Lord *endures forever.*

*"The judgments of the Lord are true and righteous
altogether."* The *judgments* of the Lord are what
results from neglect of or disobedience to the other
aspects of special revelation. If we close our eyes and
ears to the *general direction* given to us; if we scorn
the *testimonies* of the Lord; if we settle for
man-made solutions on our civic and inter-personal
relationships instead of heeding God's *statutes;* if we
disobey His specific *commandments;* and if we do not
cultivate a *fear of the Lord* — JUDGMENT is our
final destination.

The *judgments* of the Lord are true and righteous.
We may question this in our own lives and even in the
lives of others. But every time God deals, or works or
judges in the life of a man or woman — you can
know it is right. There may be a rebellious spirit
within a person that completely hinders growth.

Some of us would rather cry and stiffen our battle-line than submit.

Do you wonder why God passes judgment on His children as the need arises? One of the things that helps us to see the merciful hand of God raised in judgment is a statement from the Book of Revelation: "Lord, righteous and true are Your judgments, all the earth is being judged, but you are right, Lord, they deserve to die." In the light of this, we should cry out, "Oh, God, bring forth judgment in the earth."

I believe the words, "more to be desired are they than gold, yea, than fine gold, sweeter also than honey and the honeycomb", refer to God's judgments. Rather than go the way of developing a lawless spirit, we should say, "God, God, God, I want your judgments. I know they are righteous and true. Lord, please don't wait until I get to eternity and then reveal them to me. Deal with me now, Lord. Show it to me, God, for what it really is. Work something in my heart. More to be desired is your judgment than gold, yes, than much fine gold." He that is without judgment is without a Father!

"Moreover by them (law, testimony, statutes, commandments, fear and judgments) is thy servant warned; and in keeping of them there is great reward." We have the warning and we have the choice. We can either continue in our original *lawlessness*, or come under the judgment of the Lord and submit to His love, grace and provision. We can ask Him to put the bit and bridle and harness on us and walk along in His yoke, knowing the joy and freedom of companionship with the One who has made us for Himself; or we can go the way of the world, the end of which is death and destruction. Thank God He has given us the power of choice and clear instructions for our guidance.

Today as never before God is looking for an obedient church. And before obedience can come, we must first come to grips with our own lawless nature. I believe with all my heart that this is what God is saying to the church today. Let's listen!

Chapter Two

THE GREAT TRANSGRESSION

Picture with me, if you will, a beautiful, well-groomed German Shepherd dog, brimming with vitality and strength. He has been brought to a training school for a nine weeks' course in preparation for police duty. Lessons in obedience are necessary before he can be of any value in this assignment.

Watch the trainer as he takes a stick and throws it out into an open field with the command, "Fetch!" That great dog takes off in a cloud of dust, grabs the stick and trots back triumphantly. Then the trainer throws a purse, with the same command. Again, the trainee is off almost as soon as the purse is in the air. There is seemingly no thought of, "Should I . . . or should I not?" Instead, the immediate reaction is, "There it goes . . . here I go!"

After several runs, the officer throws the purse once more, only now he follows the act with the command, "Heel!" This requires some shifting of gears! The dog almost ruptures a blood vessel trying to follow the changed command. So many times he has "gone off" after the object, that obedience to the order to "stay" demands an act of definite effort and discipline.

Standing along the fence watching this procedure, I realized it was the most graphic illustration of OBEDIENCE I had ever seen. Relating it to some experiences God had been working out in my own life, I cried, "Oh, God, I see! I see!"

Just where do you and I fit into this picture? As children of God, the object in all of His dealings with us is to bring us into an obedient spirit.

You may ask — "What — ME — a born-again believer . . . Spirit-baptized . . . years of seeking to do God's will — is there still something for me to learn in this area of obedience?" Or you may be a comparative newcomer to the Christian way of life and searching for truths to guide you in your growth. Regardless of the circumstances, the principle involved in this matter of *obedience versus lawlessness* applies equally to us all.

To properly appreciate *obedience* in the light of God's Word, we must also investigate that other side of the coin, *lawlessness,* as presented in the Scripture. Both of these key words assume the need for commands, laws, rules and regulations which are to be used for the basis of individual decisions and attitudes. Also pictured in the two words is the ability for personal choice as to the response we will make.

The context in which we are studying this word *lawlessness,* involves a *principle,* not an outward act of lurid crime or sin. It represents the *spirit* within a person. This spirit may eventually manifest itself in open transgression, but this is only one result of harboring a lawless spirit.

Two other words used to refer to this condition of lawlessness throughout Scripture are *sin* and *iniquity.* The whole thing began with Adam and Eve and was resident in their initial disobedience and rebellion. The result of their lawlessness has continued down through the ages. Consequently, God has worked since that initial encounter with disobedience to get Himself a people from whom rebellion has been purged — a people who can say with genuine understanding, "I delight to do thy will, O God."

SCRIPTURE SPEAKS

"Not everyone that saith unto me, Lord, Lord, shall enter into the kingdom of God; but he that doeth the will of my Father which is in heaven. Many will say to me in that day, Lord, Lord, have we not prophesied in thy name? and in thy name have cast out devils? and in thy name done many wonderful works? And then I will profess unto them, I never knew (approved) you. Depart from me, ye that work *iniquity*" (Matthew 7:21–23).

"The son of man shall send forth his angels, and they shall gather out of his kingdom all things that offend, and them which do *lawlessness*" (Matthew 13:41).

"Know ye not, that to whom ye yield yourselves servants to obey, his servants ye are to whom ye obey; whether of sin unto death, or of obedience unto righteousness? But God be thanked, that ye from the heart obey, being then made free from sin, ye became the servants of righteousness. I speak after the manner of men because of the infirmity of your flesh: for as ye have yielded your members servants to uncleanness and to *lawlessness unto lawlessness:* even so now yield your members servants to righteousness unto holiness" (Romans 16:16–19). (NOTE: Lawlessness brings *more* lawlessness. This is literally the way it works.)

"The mystery of *lawlessness* doth already work" (II Thessalonians 2:7).

"For the grace of God that bringeth salvation hath appeared to all men, and it teaches us how to deny worldly lusts, looking for that blessed hope that he might redeem us from all *lawlessness* and purify unto himself a peculiar people, zealous of good works" (Titus 2:11–14). (NOTE: What is to distinguish these 'peculiar' (special) people? They have an inward desire to obey!)

"Jesus loved righteousness and hated *lawlessness;* therefore God, even thy God, hath anointed thee with the oil of gladness above thy fellows" (Hebrews 1:9).

"For I will be merciful to their unrighteousness, and their sins and their iniquities *(lawlessness)* will I remember no more" (Hebrews 8:12).

"Who gave himself for us, that he might redeem us from all *lawlessness* and purify unto himself a special people" (Titus 2:14).

We would all agree that those we refer to as being "of the world", walk in the spirit of lawlessness, for the world is rebel by nature. But what about those of us in the church? This area is not as clearly defined. Shades of lawlessness come into the church. There is a mixture – some obedience and some disobedience – sometimes we obey and sometimes we do not. If there were only some clear, distinct dividing lines, it would be easier. However, there *is* a mixture and that is what we are after. Christians need to know the answer to the question, "How much of a rebel am I?"

Also, what may have been obedience for us yesterday may be disobedience for us today. God may be trying to bring us into a new sphere of service. As the will of God is revealed, we must walk in that will as it is revealed or we will be guilty of *lawlessness*.

Do you realize, too, that we can take the truths and gifts of God and walk in disobedience? Do you see that we can actually take that which is good and make it to be rebellion and sin? Going back to the police dog, see him looking at the purse out there in the field just waiting to be retrieved. He is beginning to realize that the object isn't getting the purse — the object is obedience!

When we move ahead in our own wisdom and strength to do "our own thing", this is sin. So many of our messages and so much of our teachings has been all "go" and no "heel", that we have come to the place where most of us don't believe God would ever say, "Heel!" When we touch the power and see the need, to "heel" is hard! But I believe this is part of what God is doing in our day.

We are all familiar with the term, "general practitioner" in the field of medicine. This same term describes conditions in the church. One person may have been trying to do everything. However, the day is coming, and is here, when we are beginning to see God leading us into "specialities". If we do not listen to His directions, should He speak to us in this area, and if we continue to do all of the other things just as before, this becomes disobedience or *lawlessness*.

A DOWNWARD PATH

To help us in taking a personal inventory, Psalm 19:12–13 vividly presents five kinds of sins: "Who can understand his *errors?* Cleanse thou me from *secret faults.* Keep back thy servant also from *presumptuous sins;* let them not have *dominion* over me; then shall I be upright, and I shall be innocent from the *great transgression."*

First on the list is *errors.* The question, "Who can understand his errors?", has also been translated: "Who can tell how many times we offend?" In fact, the Psalmist might have enlarged further and asked it this way: "Who can understand how many times we must have offended God and walked off in a *lawless* spirit without even knowing it?"

When we first came to know the Lord, there probably were many things that we did and we were not even aware that the Bible said anything about it. Later, light was given to us and we realized our former ignorance. This brought responsibility for choice.

The second sin brought to our attention is *secret sin,* which falls into three categories:

(1) There is sin that is hidden to me and to others as well. It may be deeply buried, but it is a sin and God is aware of it. You may be certain He will deal with it sooner or later.

(2) Next is the sin that is hidden to others, but is is *not* hidden to me. I am aware of it but I never let anyone know about it. Yes, there are things in each of our lives that we carefully guard from exposure. There may be some pornographic literature buried in my desk drawer, or there may be some habit in which I indulge in the privacy of my own home. You would never know about it — but I am acquainted with it.

(3) Then comes the secret sin which is hidden to me but known to others. This is visible to those

around me and I am not even conscious of it. Someone may say to me, "Mumford, you are a proud rascal." To which I retort, "Me? Proud? You don't know what you are talking about!" How many of you know that if you are proud, you are usually the last one to know about it?

Or I may be accused of being stubborn. "Me, stubborn? I AM NOT STUBBORN!" This is a sin that everybody can see except *me*. I cannot see it and have a hard time believing I really am like that.

So, secret sin can take any or all of these three avenues: hidden to me and to others, but God sees; hidden to others, but known to me; hidden to me, but known to others.

Third on the downward path is *presumptuous* sin. The Hebrew word here means literally to "boil over". One certain thing about sin is that as you fool with it and continue to entertain it, something will happen inside. It starts to boil up and the next thing you know, it boils over! That pornographic literature hidden in the desk drawer, if indulged in, will finally erupt into action. That once-hidden-from-others sin is out in the open and you find yourself not caring who sees it or knows about it. That covered-up bottle of Vodka will one day rise up and assert itself and you will find yourself saying, "I'm going to drink. I don't care what people, or the church, or anyone says about it!" That is presumptuous sin.

Following close on the heels of presumptuous sin comes our fourth culprit — *dominion*. This is when you come into bondage — when you are captured by a sin and it holds you in its grasp. It can be sexual, emotional, financial, or any realm in the physical. Habits have a way of forging a chain and binding. One habit which falls into this category is smoking. A person will say, "I can get rid of cigarettes. I quit seventeen times!" And all the while he may be puffing away on the eighteenth round!

Can a Christian be in bondage? You had better believe it! The bondage can be either physical or demonic and may call for deliverance. David knew that sin is progressive in its character. He knew that if we continued walking in ignorance, the ignorant sin could develop into a secret sin if it were not discarded upon enlightenment. Then that secret sin could come to a boiling point and grow into presumption. Finally — dominion comes onto the scene!

Notice that David says at the closing of verse 13: "... and I shall be innocent of the *great transgression.*" Here we make a difference between the first four sins and the fifth one. All sin is related to rebellion. They are first cousins. However, rebellion is a special kind of sin in its own category. You can be free from error, secret sin, presumptuousness and dominion and still have rebellion in your spirit. In fact, some of the most rebellious people outwardly display an image exactly the opposite of any man-made picture of rebellion. This is why we need to probe deeply right here.

In our first four instances, sin is a matter of *conduct.* These are evidenced in the way you and I conduct our lives. There is an element of rebellion in them — but our fifth sin is an *attitude* and this is harder to deal with than conduct. The first four groupings of sins can be and are forgiven when confessed. However, when you enter into the realm of rebellion — this represents a different condition and leads into a situation where you may become *irredeemable!* There is nothing more that God can do when rebellion has worked its full cycle except execute judgment. Let me repeat — when rebellion has completed its work and you are a full-grown rebel . . . self-willed . . . incorrigible . . . unchangeable — this is *the great transgression — the spirit of rebellion!*

HOW CAN I KNOW?

How can I know if I am a rebel? It is only fair to give some ways to determine whether or not you and I are rebels.

Some of us came into the church fighting. We may have grown up in surroundings that bred a rebellious attitude. Perhaps we learned in our formative years to fight our way through life and came to feel this was the only way to get along in our world. When we were introduced to Jesus, we took those attitudes, sanctified them, put Bible texts on them and steam-rolled ahead saying, "You get out of the way. I'm going to serve Jesus!! I don't care what you do, but I'm going all the way!!" I speak from experience. Here is proof that "out of the heart the mouth speaketh." Do you see the difference between conduct and attitude?

Checking the word "rebellion" in the Bible can be a mind-blowing experience. Warnings against this attitude and the results of continuing in this condition are splattered across the entire history of Israel. Two instances which help us understand this condition and the heartbreak it caused God are:

Isaiah 1:2 — "I have brought forth many children but they rebelled against me . . . the ass knows its stall but my people don't even know who their God is."

Zechariah 7:11 — "But they refused to hearken, and pulled away the shoulder . . ." Do you get the picture here? Those of you who have children know very well this response. You try to talk to one of them, ''Honey, let me tell you something . . .'' — and they pull away from you in anger. That is *attitude,* Church. It is deeper than conduct. It is something that goes down into the fiber of the being. The literal translation of Israel's response to God's attempt to talk to them goes like this: "We will come no more unto thee. We are lords!"

Then in I Samuel 15:17–31 there is the dramatic scene involving the prophet Samuel and King Saul which we are going to use as a basis in our search for answers to this question, "Am I a rebel?"

(17) "And Samuel said, When thou was little in thine own sight (here is an attitude) *was thou not made the head of the tribes of Israel, and the Lord anointed thee king over Israel?*

(18) "And the Lord sent thee on a journey and said, (Now this is a commandment, and the commandments of the Lord are always clear) *Go and utterly destroy the sinners, the Amalekites, and fight against them until they are consumed.*

(19) "Wherefore then didst thou not obey the voice of the Lord, but didst fly upon the spoil, and didst evil in the sight of the Lord? (Here we have the disobedient act of Saul.)

(20) "And Saul said unto Samuel, Yea, I have obeyed the voice of the Lord (keep this response in mind) *and have gone the way which the Lord sent*

me, and have brought Agag the king of Amalek, and have utterly destroyed the Amalekites.

(21) "But the people (here is the second reply to keep in mind) *took the spoil, sheep and oxen, the chief of the things which should have been utterly destroyed, to sacrifice unto the Lord thy God in Gilgal.*

(22) "And Samuel said, Hath the Lord as great delight in all your burnt offerings and sacrifices, as in obeying the voice of the Lord?"

It is still so much easier today, as it was for Saul in his situation, to bring "burnt offerings and sacrifices" than to obey the clear command of the Lord. Church attendance . . . president of the vestry . . . helping to buy new organs, song books, new pads for the pews — these all require much less sacrifice than does actual outright obedience to a clear command of the Lord. Especially is this so, when the command demands giving up something we are holding dear, even though we may know it is expressly in violation to His will.

One day God had me in a tight place. The Red Sea seemed to be in front of me — mountains on each side — and Pharoah coming up in the rear. I was crying and weeping and the Lord said, "Mumford . . ."

"Yes, Lord?" I wailed.

"When you are all done crying, how about obeying?"

He had me right there!

(23) "For rebellion is as the sin of witchcraft, and stubbornness is as iniquity and idolatry. Because thou hast rejected the word of the Lord, he hath also rejected thee from being king." (Judgment!).

Rebellion is an attitude! Why didn't God just forgive Saul? Can you see that Saul's disobedience in this case clearly revealed his rebellious attitude? God gives us a command — and we disobey; but we realize our disobedience and ask God to forgive us. He does because there is not YET a rebellious attitude.

But persistent disobedience *leads* to a rebellious attitude! This is where we need to stop, look and listen. One thing I have learned about God is that after a first disobedience, the second time the Lord gives a command, His voice is softer. I may reason — "Well, the Lord has forgiven me." However, the time following there may only be a whispered command. I have discovered when His voice becomes softer in giving the commands, it means that He is leaving — we are not getting away with something! God has a way of recognizing and revealing our attitudes to us.

This you may not like to hear! Rebellion . . . witchcraft . . . demonizing! In our day in the United States of America we are in a witchcraft revival. Pagan lands have already had their witchcraft revivals. What is the root of it all? Why are people turning to astrology and the occult in such overwhelming numbers? Why are colleges offering credit courses in this subject? The truth is this: as we find ourselves in a rebellious attitude, we open the whole inner nature of our being to all kinds of demon activity. This is true of our children and our entire society today. Hasn't rebellion been a keynote in our society on an ever-increasing scale?

Let me ask you another straight question. Did this happen in Saul's life? This man who was called of

God, anointed and presented with every opportunity to serve his people in his day — what developed from his disobedient and rebellious attitude? The end result was demonizing and then that ultimate cop-out — suicide! There is also a remarkable revival of suicide in our day. Most people who take this route would rather give up their lives than obey. So strong is the spirit of rebellion!

(24) "And Saul said unto Samuel, I have sinned; for I have transgressed the commandment of the Lord, (Saul knew very well that he had disobeyed) *and thy words: because I feared the people, and obeyed their voice.*

(25) "Now therefore, I pray thee, pardon my sin, and turn again with me, that I may worship the Lord.

(26) "And Samuel said unto Saul, I will not return with thee for thou hast rejected the word of the Lord, and the Lord hath rejected thee from being king over Israel. (Note that Saul's soul was not lost for eternity. This is a matter of judgment — rejection from the place of responsibility to which he had been called.)

(27) "And as Samuel turned about to go away, he laid hold upon the skirt of his mantle and it rent.

(28) "And Samuel said unto him, the Lord hath rent the kingdom of Israel from thee this day, and hath given it to a neighbor of thine, that is better than thou.

(29) "Also the Strength of Israel will not lie nor repent; for he is not a man, that he should repent.

(30) "Then he said, I have sinned; yet honour me now, I pray thee, before the elders of my people, and before Israel and turn again with me, that I may worship the Lord thy God."

Here is one way in which we can judge whether or not we are a rebel. What was Saul worried about? Public opinion! He wanted to walk into "church" once more so that the people would not know about his situation. Samuel agreed. But he might have added, "It isn't going to change anything!"

(31) "So Samuel turned again after Saul; and Saul worshiped the Lord."

IT'S UP TO YOU

After reading the story of Saul, you may be asking, "How can I tell whether my disobedience is one of the first four sins — error, secret sin, presumptuous sin, dominion — *or* if it is the attitude of rebellion?" And certainly this is what we need to discover.

This is a day of using abbreviations and the first letters of proper names or titles in order to save time . . . IBM . . . JFK . . . IRS . . . KJV . . . and others. Let me give you another threesome to add to your list — V.R.G. These letters play a part in the way you can determine if you are a rebel or not. If you throw around V.R.G. (and that stands for *Verbalized Religious Garbage!*), you had better make out a check list and get busy!

When you are faced with disobedience on your part and God puts the "stone of offense" right in your path, you have the choice of four attitudes you can assume. Saul had these four choices. As we consider them, we get some answers to our question, "Am I a rebel?".

1. What did Saul say when Samuel asked the question in verse 19: "Wherefore then didst thou not

obey the voice of the Lord . . .?" He began at once to come up with some V.R.G. . . . "I have obeyed."

Someone comes to me and says, "Brother Mumford, I don't know why I am so sick. My home is in utter confusion . . . my marriage is breaking up . . . things are in a terrible state."

"Did you obey the Lord?" I ask.

"Oh, yes! I have kept the commandments from my youth up."

"Never did anything wrong?"

"Never — Oh, no — not me!"

Does this response have a familiar ring to it?

2. The second response is almost the same — more V.R.G. Only this time Saul tries another escape mechanism, "The people did it!" Instead of admitting, "I didn't obey", he continued evading and now blamed it on someone else. I wonder what God would have done if Saul had been man enough to have said, "You know — I didn't obey — and there is a rebellious spirit in me. Once I was humble and now I am not. Samuel, I need help!"

3. The third choice is the one that leads to the point of no return. The first response is trying to get around it; the second one is blaming it on somebody else; but here the person says, "I can't face it." Isn't it tragic that at times we would rather turn back than admit we are wrong? We insist, "The Lord has been too hard on me. I can't continue in this discipleship thing — it's too tough." Your rebellion remains intact. Nothing can touch you. You have no intention of changing your life style. God cannot break that *core* of rebellion that lies at the center of your being and is causing your trouble. Remember *sin* is what you do. Rebellion is the result of *what you are.*

4. Finally, we have the fourth choice — that of being broken — of saying, "God, you are looking at a rebel. God, I need help. God, I want you to break that thing that is inside — that thing that exalts itself against Your will." When this attitude is reached, God says, "O.K., I'll fix you up."

For a classic example of our fourth choice, we look at an incident in the life of King David, the man who was chosen to replace King Saul after his rejection by God. Do you know what I believe about David? I believe he was just as much a rebel as Saul. But, oh, the difference when David was faced with the "stone of offence" in his life by God.

David had a strong spirit. He had what the modern youth would call, "real power under the hood!" When he wanted something he got it. Recall how he went up on the housetop and looking over he saw beautiful Bathsheba. His immediate reaction was, "I think I'd like to have her. Find out who she is and bring her to me." He was king and got most anything he wanted! But God did not let David get away with his sinning in taking another man's wife and having her husband killed. Just as Samuel confronted Saul with his disobedience, so God used another prophet to bring before David the enormity of his sin.

Listen to Nathan as he tells David the parable about a rich man who had many flocks and herds and then took the one little ewe lamb of the poor man (II Samuel 12). David's anger sparked at the injustice and he cried, "Who is that man? I'll have his head roll!" That shows something of the spirit of the man. Now when God got David in a corner and through Nathan revealed the truth — "Thou art the man — wherefore hast thou despised the commandment of the Lord, to do evil in his sight . . .?", what did David do?

The great King David took our fourth choice — no V.R.G. here — he broke! He said, "God, that is right. I am the man!" Do you know that David could have offered God five hundred bulls as a sacrifice for his sin? However, the core of rebellion would have remained intact.

Let me ask: is it possible that when we are faced with a sin, we may try to satisfy ourselves by saying, "The blood of Jesus cleanses me from all sin." At the same time, we may have no intention of giving up that particular sin. We may also say, "I just want to be forgiven, I don't want to change." Do you see that this is not a matter of merely asking for forgiveness for a certain sinful *act?* It is a matter of breaking. The Christian life is not a series of forgivenesses, it is a series of changes. It is not just the disobedience that needs to be taken care of — it is a matter of attitude. Attitude is deeper than sin. One translation of Psalm 51:17 that brings home something of what is involved in breaking is: "The sacrifice of God is a soul with its evil crushed."

Notice it is the evil that is crushed — not the soul or spirit. I have seen people under the dealings of God who give the appearance of complete defeat. They are all bent over and dragged out — completely without any joy or vitality. To the question, "How are you doing?", their reply goes something like this: "Just waiting to go to heaven . . . this life is too hard on me . . soon the Lord is going to take me out of it all." Do you realize that this, too, is a form of V.R.G.? Trying to give the impression of our maturity can sometimes be a smokescreen for the truth that God is at work trying to break the core of a rebellious spirit.

How about going back with me to our opening illustration and taking another look at that police dog going through his paces?

While watching the training, one thing deeply impressed me. Something that *must not happen* was this: the dog's spirit could not be broken. If that dog had come out with his tail hanging between his legs and with his ears drooping when his trainer said, "Go get the purse!", what kind of testimony would that have been to the desired finished product – a beautifully trained and obedient dog? This is not what God wants from us, either.

A broken spirit is not one that says, "Oh, God, not again!" It does not project the picture of a life filled with self-pity or one that enjoys a groveling and grumbling level of living. The "poor me" attitude is just V.R.G. Instead there must be an attitude which displays joy, praise and confidence in God's workings.

I have learned that when the Lord says, "Sit" – "Run" – "Heel", to *ZIP* – sit, run and heel! Ears up! Life is wonderful! Glory to God! I have also learned that when He says, "Roll over!", not to growl at Him, but to roll over! You just can't beat a dog in that position! Two more lessons that I have been taught are: (1) the more I obey, the more complete is my joy; (2) every time I go my own way, I get into trouble.

We must remember in this matter of learning, that God is going to continue stedfast in His love, but He will deal with us and judge us according to our needs. He may have to take away His anointing for service and give it to another, as He did in the case of Saul and David. God's will and work goes on, even though at times His servants have to be "put out to pasture" due to disobedience or rebellion.

David was a different man after his "breaking". The Psalms attested to this. Hear him say, "I will sing of mercy and judgment: unto thee, O Lord, will I sing . . . Serve the Lord with gladness; come before his presence with singing . . . Surely goodness and mercy shall follow me all the days of my life and I shall dwell in the house of the Lord forever!"

This is the result toward which the Lord continues to work. He desires a people who can say from a heart overflowing with love and gratitude, "I delight to do thy will, O, God." We *can* know if we are rebels and if we are "innocent of the great transgression."

Chapter Three
ANTIDOTE TO REBELLION

If there were to be an open contest today for the MAN MOST LIKELY NOT TO SUCCEED as a proponent of current ethics, my candidate would be the *Apostle Paul.* Does this surprise you? However, on one plank alone (and there are others), he would, I believe, carry the vote of the majority as being extremely unpopular, if not almost totally unacceptable. What is that one plank? *"Let Every Soul Be Subject Unto the Higher Powers!" (Romans 13:1a).*

What do those eight simple one-and-two-syllable words do to you? Does the hair on the back of your neck stand up as you think about being subject to *anyone* — must less to powers in all of the three main arenas of life: the spiritual — the civil — the home.

Rebellion is probably the fastest growing element in our society today. It pervades every area of existence. Age, sex, temperment, situation — there seems to be no barrier to stop its onrush. What does this reveal to the sensitive eye and listening ear? Can man's basic sinful nature be hurtling him to self-destruction? Where does God fit into this picture? Never fear . . . God is here . . . He is right on center stage! In fact, He had the antidote to rebellion even before man first rebelled. His eternal task has been getting man to recognize and accept the divine remedy.

LISTEN TO GOD!

The Old Testament tells us of God's desire and efforts to enter into a covenant relationship with His people, working through the Jewish race. Centuries of dealings proved beyond a doubt the inability of man to keep his part of the covenant. God knew this would be the outcome. But He needed to reveal the inevitable to all people, causing them to come to Him for His provision.

Hear God as He speaks through the Prophet Jeremiah to the people of his day — (Jeremiah 31:31—34).

(31) "Behold, the days come, saith the Lord, that I will make a new covenant with the house of Israel, and with the house of Judah.

(32) "It won't be the same as the covenant that I made with their fathers in the day that I took them by the hand to bring them out of the land of Egypt; which my covenant they broke, although I was an husband unto them, saith the Lord:

(33) "But this shall be the covenant that I will make with the house of Israel: After those days, saith the Lord, I will put my law in their inward parts, and I will write it in their hearts; and I will be their God, and they shall be my people.

(34) "And they shall teach no more every man his neighbour, and every man his brother, saying, Know the Lord; for they shall all know me, from the least of them unto the greateast of them, saith the Lord,

for I will forgive their lawlessness, and I will remember their sin no more."

In the New Testament (Hebrews 8:7–13), God again presents the need for a new covenant, stressing the reason for this divine replacement. God's stratagies are always paced to man's responses.

(7) "For if that first covenant had been faultless, then should no place have been sought for the second.

(8) "For finding fault with them, he saith, Behold the days come, saith the Lord, when I will make a new covenant with the house of Israel and with the house of Judah:

(9) "Not according to the covenant that I made with their fathers in the day when I took them by the hand to lead them out of the land of Egypt; because they continued not in my covenant, and I rejected (or disapproved) *them and I regarded them not, saith the Lord.*

(10) "For this is the covenant that I will make with the house of Israel after those days, saith the Lord: I will put my laws into their mind and write them in their hearts; and I will be to them a God, and they shall be to me a people.

(11) "And they shall not teach every man his neighbour, and every man his brother, saying, Know the Lord: for all shall know me, from the least to the greatest.

(12) "For I will be merciful to their unrighteousness, and their iniquities will I remember no more.

(13) "In that he saith, a new covenant, he hath made the first old. Now that which decayeth and waxeth old is ready to vanish away."

I have written the word *Exasperation* alongside this next portion — Isaiah 5:1—7. Here God plainly and forcibly presents His side of the story, telling how His every energy had been expended toward the desired goal of bringing unto Himself a people in a love-relationship. Do you detect heartbreak in verse 4? "I don't know what else to do. I have done everything that I know how to do."

(1) "Now will I sing to my well-beloved a song of my beloved touching his vineyard. My well-beloved hath a vineyard in a very fruitful hill:

(2) "And he fenced it, and gathered out the stones thereof, and planted it with the choicest vine (what does John 15 say about the Vine?) *and built a tower in the midst of it, and also made a winepress therein: and he looked that it should bring forth grapes, and it brought forth wild grapes.*

(3) "And now, O inhabitants of Jerusalem, and men of Judah, judge, I pray you, between me and my vineyard.

(4) "What could have been done more to my vineyard, that I have not done to it? Wherefore, when I looked that it should bring forth grapes, brought it forth wild grapes?

(5) "And now go to: I will tell you what I will do to my vineyard: I will take away the hedge thereof, and it shall be eaten up; and break down the wall thereof, and it shall be trodden down:

(6) "And I will lay it waste, it shall not be pruned, nor digged, but there shall come up briers and thorns: I will also command the clouds that they rain no rain upon it.

(7) "For the vineyard of the Lord of hosts is the house of Israel, and the men of Judah his pleasant

plant: and he looked for judgment, but behold oppression; for righteousness, but behold a cry."

GRAPES OR LEAVES?

What was wrong with the people of the Old Covenant? A lot of religion but no obedience! Inside was that rebellious core which, when unbroken, results in the great transgression — and ultimate rejection insofar as effective usefulness in the Kingdom goes. God tells Israel, "I am looking for fruit and all I get is wild grapes." Jesus had something to say on this matter, also — Luke 20:9—18:

(9) "Then began he to speak to the people this parable: A certain man planted a vineyard, and let it forth to husbandmen, and went into a far country for a long time.

(10) "And at the season he sent a servant to the husbandmen, that they should give him of the fruit of the vineyard; but the husbandmen beat him, and sent him away empty.

(11) "And again he sent another servant: and they beat him also, and entreated him shamefully, and sent him away empty.

(12) "And again he sent a third: and they wounded him also, and cast him out.

(13) "Then said the lord of the vineyard, what shall I do? I will send my beloved son: it may be that they will reverence him when they see him.

(14) "But when the husbandmen saw him, they reasoned among themselves saying, This is the heir: come, let us kill him, that the inheritance may be ours.

(15) "*So they cast him out of the vineyard, and killed him. What therefore shall the lord of the vineyard do unto them?*

(16) "*He shall come and destroy these husbandmen, and shall give the vineyard to others, and when they heard it, they said, God forbid* (They knew what Jesus was predicting).

(17) "*And he beheld them, and said, What is this then that is written, The stone which the builders rejected, the same is become head of the corner?*

(18) "*Whosoever shall fall upon that stone shall be broken: but on whomsoever it shall fall, it will grind him to powder.*"

May I introduce you to one of the distinctions between the old covenant and the new? The problem God was dealing with here was the complacency and sense of "having arrived" which had settled over the Jews. They asserted proudly, "We are the people! God could never reject us!" The prophets warned that God would judge them for this attitude. They proclaimed in no uncertain words that God would make a new covenant and it would not have within it the same problem. Jesus, too, warned them.

Matthew 21:43 records: "Therefore say I unto you, the Kingdom of God shall be taken from you, and given to a nation bringing forth the fruits thereof." And that is exactly what God did. He took the kingdom from them and gave it to the early church. As the people of the new covenant moved down through the developing years, whenever the cry went out; "We are the people!", God's reply remained constant — "No one will ever again be able to say, 'We are the people'!" God is still looking for grapes.

The Roman church, the Crusaders, the Protestant Movement, the Wesleyans, the Pentecostals — it does not take very long for any group to fall into this condition. Liturgies . . . great cathedrals with their stained glass windows . . . 700 missionaries on the field . . . our budget bigger than last year — do you catch the undertone of "We are the People!"? No one is going to make this claim unchallenged. God moves in upon our "empires" saying, "If there are no grapes, I will take the thing that makes grapes (the anointing) and find someone whose desire it is to grow grapes — not leaves."

A wise teacher once advised me regarding a particular movement, "This is a wonderful work but it is beginning to sink. Now if this thing sinks, don't sink with it. Get off and get on something that is floating!" It is easy to be so committed to a *thing* that you go right down iwth it. When the death knoll starts ringing, that proclaims the time for the Master of the Vineyard to return, pick up the thing that makes grapes and take it on to someone else. Nobody can stop that. It happens to groups, denominations and individuals. Let me share with you a spiritual secret — don't be impressed with the leaves. Look through them and ask, "Where are the grapes?" Another secret? The key is obedience . . . "Doing the will of My Father!"

THE PRUNING HOOK

We have seen the danger in assuming, "We are the people!"; along with the strain of rebellion and lack of fruit-bearing, which are inherent in this attitude. Now let me show you another explosive truth as unveiled by Jesus in His remarks to the scribes and Pharisees — Matthew 23:28—24:2. Here is the razor-sharp edge of the pruning hook.

(28) "Even so ye also outwardly appear righteous unto men (phylacteries, prayer beads, skull caps — defenders of God's honor!) *but within ye are full of hypocrisy and iniquity* (play-acting and lawlessness).

(29) "Woe unto you, scribes and Pharisees, hypocrites! because ye build the tombs of the prophets, and garnish the sepulchres of the righteous (statues to John Calvin . . . new church to honor Martin Luther . . . we call our church Knox Presbyterian!);

(30) "And say, If we had been in the days of our fathers, we would not have been partakers with them in the blood of the prophets (if we had been living in the days of Martin Luther, would we have been right in there signing the death warrants? In the days of Azusa Street, would we have been throwing tomatoes along with the rest of them?)

(31) "Wherefore ye be witnesses unto yourselves, that ye are the children of them which killed the prophets.

(32) "Fill ye up then the measure of your fathers.

(33) "Ye serpents, ye generation of vipers, how can ye escape the damnation of hell?

(34) "Wherefore, behold, I send unto you prophets, and wise men, and scribes: and some of them ye shall kill and crucify: and some of them shall ye scourge in your synagoges, and persecute them from city to city:

(35) "That upon you may come all the righteous blood shed upon the earth, from the blood of

righteous Abel unto the blood of Zacharias son of Barachias, whom ye slew between the temple and the altar.

(36) "Verily I say unto you, All these things shall come upon this generation.

(37) "O Jerusalem, Jerusalem, thou that killest the prophets, and stonest them which are sent unto thee, how often would I have gathered thy children together, even as a hen gathereth her chickens under her wings, and ye would not! (Saddest words in the Bible! Do you see an atttiude here? Do you see an incorrigible, unchangeable, crystalized religious attitude that would not bend or break?).

(38) "Behold, your house (Herod's temple − that mighty building where the Shekinah of Glory was resting) *is left unto you desolate.*

(39) "For I say unto you, Ye shall not see me henceforth, till ye shall say, Blessed is he that cometh in the name of the Lord.

(24:1) "And Jesus went out (He left that "thing" − all that was spiritual and real, got up and walked out and all they had left was a religious club): *and his disciples came to him for to shew him the buildings of the temple* (Master, you are making a mistake − leaving this beautiful building . . . $50,000 organ . . .):

(2) "And Jesus said unto them, See ye not all these things? Verily I say unto you, There shall not be left here one stone upon another, that shall not be thrown down."

I want these next thoughts to burn into our hearts. What was the final thing that made Jesus leave the temple? It was not the hypocrisy of his day, or adultery, or bank-robbing, or gambling − it was *how they treated His servants!* Rebellion is consummated by the way we treat God's servants. God manifests our rebellion by putting someone directly over us and putting us under authority. Rejection of delegated authority results in removal of the anointing — the glory — that "thing" that makes grapes.

Do you know what God is saying to the Church? One dynamic word sums it up — *Submission.* What was it Paul said in Romans 13:1 that makes him even today a prober into the depths of our beings? *"Let every man be subject unto the higher powers."* Do you question his popularity?

Going back to the parable Jesus told in Luke 20, recall: "There is a certain man who made a vineyard. And when it came time to collect the grapes from it, he sent them a servant. They beat the servant and threw him out of the vineyard and said, 'Who do you think you are?' So he sent another one and they did the same thing. Finally the master of the vineyard said, 'You know something, I will send them my son and when they see him, they will honor him.' But when the son came, they said, 'Aha, here is the heir. We will kill him and take the whole inheritance.' So they cast him out of the vineyard and killed him."

RECEIVE — OR ELSE!

We may not like to hear that command, "Submit", but ultimate rebellion is revealed by how we react to God's delegated authority. Do you know that is what I am, delegated authority — a servant entrusted with responsibilities. I was a sailor, having a good time, when God said to me, "Mumford, I want you." My unbelieving reply was, "You do?" Not only I, but many of my friends, thought this was God's first mistake! But when I accepted God's call to the ministry, I determined that my one purpose in life would be to stand honest, true and open in His presence — an obedient and willing servant.

Let me share with you an experience I had early in my ministry. I was invited to take part in a convention in Peru. Assignment was made for me to go to the home of a Peruvian family. As you know, poverty there is indescribable. When I walked into that humble home, here was a little table set like the Waldorf-Astoria and beside it was *one* chair. All kinds of foods were heaped on that table and the family was standing around it. I said, "When are we going to eat?"

My host replied in his broken English, "Oh, brother, we don't eat. The man of God is here."

The reverent tone of his voice made me want to turn around to see if Elijah had come up behind me. I asked, "What do you eat?"

"Oh, we don't eat while the man of God is here. We will eat whatever you leave." So, with father, mother, and nine children lined up around the wall, I sat down and tried to eat. I almost choked and the food turned to paste in my mouth. Tears dripped into the plate. All the while they were thanking God, worshipping the Lord and saying, "Oh God, we thank you that you have honored our house and sent to us a man of God."

Something began to break inside of me and I cried, "God, how this must please You that they would so esteem the man of God." I sensed the very pleasure of Jesus resting on the gathering. This was not hero worship. It was something they had learned. Here was

a man of God who had come into thier home and
they were receiving His servant as they would have
received Him!

Now, if you can catch in this one statement, made
by Jesus, the same truth that dawned on me, your
entire spiritual perspective can be revolutionized.
"Blessed is he that comes in the name of the Lord"
(Matthew 23:29). What I saw altered many
relationships in my life. Jesus is telling us that He and
His servants are so inextricably intertwined that they
cannot be separated. Until I can learn to say, "Blessed
is he who comes *to me* in the name of the Lord", I
will never really understand what the Lord is doing in
the earth. I must *learn* to submit to those who have
authority over me.

In our generation many are saying, "We don't
believe in leadership — in authority — in pastors,
and all that. We are spiritual. We have no head but
Jesus." Try feeling through the leaves — any grapes?
True, there may be a lot of things going on. There
may be excitement. But turn to Matthew 10:40 and
see what God has ordained: "He that receiveth you
receiveth me, and he that receiveth me receiveth him
that sent me."

Do you detect what God has in mind? Christ puts
Himself one step behind the man of God, and His
Father is one step behind Him. Then He says, "I am
going to watch to see how you treat my servant. You
treat him right and I will come to you. My Father is
right behind Me. You reject my servant — goodbye,
I'll see you later." Verse 41 continues: "He that
receiveth a prophet in the name (or office) of a
prophet, shall receive a prophet's reward; and he that
receiveth a righteous man in the name of a righteous

man shall receive a righteous man's reward." Are you beginning to see why the Lord put Himself one step behind the man of God?

To illustrate, let me use a family situation. I have two sons, ages ten and four. The one is trying to help his brother get ready for bed. The older says, "Put on your pajamas."

To which the younger retorts, "I don't have to!"

Next attempt, "Yes, you do. I'm your brother and you had better listen to me."

Second comeback, "I don't have to mind you. I'm getting big myself."

In the midst of the fighting back and forth, father comes onto the scene. "What's going on in here?" (Suddenly my younger son becomes amazingly docile.) "You had better obey your brother."

"Yessir, I will . . . I will!" But as soon as I leave the room it begins all over again . . ."I don't have to obey you!" Father, yes — brother, — no!

Truth flashed across my mind. We will gladly say, "I want God to rule over me!" We feel safe because God is far removed from the scene of action. But when it comes to obeying delegated authority, the man of God — that pastor . . . police officer . . . husband . . . parent — what a different story!

Let's say God calls me to a particular assignment. I agree to go. He says, "When you get there, some people will refuse you and others will receive you. Those who refuse you, refuse Me." Do you see that if you refuse me, I cannot minister to you? If you reject me, I cannot help you? Some people accept me as a teacher. Others have a somewhat different opinion! However, was this same thing true of Jesus? Is it true that when they rejected Him, they rejected His ministry? Was it true of Paul? In some places they said, "The man of God has come." In other places they scornfully threw him out of their synagogues. Those who turned their backs and stopped their ears never entered into that new day that was breaking in upon their world. When Paul was received, eyes were opened.

Take another of Jesus' teachings — Luke 10:16 — "He that heareth you heareth me; and he that despiseth you despiseth me; and he that despiseth me despiseth him that sent me." When God calls His servants and they accept the call, the two are involved together in ministry. If the servant is rejected, that is part of the package! Misunderstanding and rejection may come. The servant stands as a question mark in the test of rebellion.

God may say to me, "I am sending you to Timbuktu to test their rebellion. If the rebellion is broken in them, they will receive you. If not, their attitude closes the door to effective ministry." Do you know why it seems to you that God sends you servants who rub you the wrong way — ones you think don't know how to preach — some who don't seem "to have it all put together yet"? Could you be needing to say, "Blessed is he who comes *to me* in the name of the Lord"? There may be clenched teeth as you say, "I love you, pastor. . . I love you, elder. . . I am going to love you if it kills me!" In doing this you are saying to rebellion, "Die, you rascal, die!" Death to rebellion comes slowly, but in it you learn to embrace that one, and truthfully say, "Blessed is he . . ."

In my own life, as soon as I was able to assume this attitude, the Lord began to send men into my life who understood what God was doing. As soon as I could honestly say, "Blessed are the men that come to me in the name of the Lord . . . Lord, I receive that man," suddenly there was Jesus standing right behind that man saying, "Son, I have something to say to you." *And I could hear!*

THE DIVINE FORMULA

To help us better understand the principle we have just shared, we take several portions of Scripture. These present a concept that will further reveal the spiritual nature of the authority of Christ.

II Corinthians 5:16 — "Wherefore henceforth know we no man after the flesh: yea, though we have known Christ after the flesh, yet henceforth know we him no more." The historical Christ, born of a virgin, having a phsycial body just as we do, — this was Jesus Who walked the shores of Galilee. Some poeple today are worshiping *only* that Jesus . . . and all the while there is a resurrected Christ Who has given Himself to us. Jesus came to earth to do the will of God. In that will was the cross of Calvary, the tomb, and the resurrection. Later the Son of God ascended to sit on the right hand of the Father. He Who ascended, also descended and gave Himself to men through His gifts . . . fruit . . . authority.

In John 16:14—16, we find Jesus preparing His disciples for this very development:

(14) "He (the Holy Spirit) *shall glorify me: for he shall receive of mine, and shall shew it unto you.*

(15) "All things that the Father hath are mine:

therefore said I, that he shall take of mine, and shall shew it unto you.

(16) "A little while, and ye shall not see me: and again, a little while, and ye shall see me: because I go to the Father."

Paraphrasing these verses may help us get the message which He was unfolding, "I, Jesus, am going to the Father; and when I go to the Father, the Holy Spirit, in my name, will take the things that belong to me — that is the gifts of the Spirit, the fruit of the Spirit and the authority (apostles, prophets, pastors, teachers, evangelists) and give it all to the church. And when the Holy Spirit is come, dividing to the church these gifts and ministries of the Spirit, *you will see Me!*

Our third reference is Ephesians 1:22—23.

(Perhaps a diagram will enable us to better grasp this transition as shown forth in these scriptures).

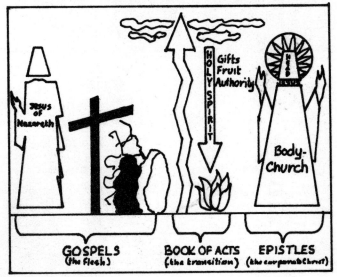

(22) "And hath put all things under his feet, and gave him to be the head over all things to the church,

(23) "Which is his body, the fulness of him that filleth all in all."

First we have the Christ whom we knew after the flesh. That is Jesus Who walked the shores of Galilee. He told us, "If I go away, I will come to you." We do not worship Him after the flesh anymore, Paul said in II Corinthians 5:16. In the Book of Acts we saw the coming of the Holy Spirit and founding of the church which experienced the fulfillment of Jesus' promise, "Ye shall receive power!"

Then we have Christ, the Head, and those of us who believe on His name, the Body. We must come to understand that the Body is the gifts and ministries and operations of the Spirit. This is the corporate Christ. When we see this, we have new appreciation for the many-membered body, made up of all fellow believers. Now my wife is no longer "just my wife". She is a member of the body of Christ. Also, I have a different respect for my borhter as a member of the body of Christ. If we do not esteem a man and recognize his place and part in the body, we are looking at him only as a man after the flesh.

APPLYING THE PRESCRIPTION

When is that rebellious spirit in me going to be broken and its leaven purged out of my life? God says, "I'll tell you when. If you really want to see Me and comprehend what I am doing in the earth, learn to say, 'Blessed is he who comes in the name of the Lord'!"

He also says, "Let every soul be subject unto the

higher powers." When we learn to submit to our immediate superiors – our pastor . . . elder . . . husband . . . school teacher – suddenly we will find something breaking on the inside and our eyes will begin to open to see God's purpose and plan. We will see His spiritual body, and the kingdom of God, and what He is doing.

You can never bring in God's kingdom by rebellion. Your "higher power" may not be "doing it right", according to your standards; but your responsibility then is to take him or her before the Lord and ask Him to deal in the matter. There is not a thing you can do about it but submit. You can get mad at God, you can go off on your own, you can initiate a personal search; however, in the long run, you have to find somebody to whom you can say, "Blessed is he that comes in the name of the Lord."

Jesus laid down the principle – "You won't see Me anymore until you *learn* to say that." And believe me, this does not come naturally. We all have to *learn* this lesson. Even Jesus learned obedience by the things which He suffered. It may cause suffering. In fact, it probably will. But the antidote to rebellion is plainly spelled out. We are given instructions as to how to apply the formula. He gave us the assistance of the Holy Spirit to administer the prescription. However – here is the catch!

In every area of life man is a free moral agent. God made him that way. The responsibility for taking advantage of what has been provided *for him* is up *to him*. Do you recall David's attitude toward King Saul? "I dare not touch God's anointed" (I Samuel 26:9). David had every opportunity to kill Saul – but He respected God's delegated authority.

And I dare not turn away in rebellion from that one whom God has put over me without incurring possible blindness and deafness to spiritual truth.

Let me ask you another question. Did you know that the highest form of worship is obedience? Jesus' statement, "You will not see Me any more until you . . . submit!", plows deep. We may not like this antidote to rebellion any better than we may like accepting a certain prescribed remedy for combating a fatal physical illness. Remember, God's medication carries a Life-guarantee. The wide open road to full recovery stretches out ahead. It is yours for the taking!

Chapter Four

UNDERSTANDING SPIRITUAL AUTHORITY

Each of the above three words — *Understanding — Spiritual — Authority* — is a study in itself. Put them all together, they add up to *DYNAMITE!* But as I travel across our land, and in many other nations, this is what I hear God saying to the Body everywhere. Could it be that He is moving us into territory marked: *DANGER, GOD AT WORK!*

Would you agree with me that these words, taken both on an individual basis and as a concept, picture a progressive and developmental process? We are familiar with the phrases, "clothed with authority" and "the voice of authority". What are some of the sights and sounds we have come to associate with that s o m e t i m e s a w e s o m e . . . s o m e t i m e s welcomed . . . even at times, terrifying word — *authority?*

What about the infant? Shortly after experiencing the warmth and security of mother's arms and the sound of father's laughter, there come new and different feelings and sounds. Among the first of these to impress the mind and form reactings, are the words, "no . . . no". Yes, early he learns there are some "no — no" areas in his little world. Early he begins to form responses to this puzzling situation — his own desires and that voice and word which carries a discordant sound, even to his limited understanding.

As the years pass, hopefully, there would be a

growing feeling of love and acceptance in his family circle and his expanding world. There comes conditioning, instruction and example in the meaning of, and need for, the "no — no's" of life. "Daddy says so .,. ." brings a recognition of authority and its expected obedience. Also, it brings the realization of possible disobedience and resulting consequences.

Soon other "authorities" appear on the scene. Not only parents, but brother . . . sister . . . teachers . . . policeman . . . the man at the grocery store . . . all seem to possess this choice-making formula. There are written, as well as verbal, signposts along the way. Even self-formed mental projections throw up questions and answers.

Can you see that when God is brought into one's awareness, already thought patterns are formed . . . consciousness of choice has become a part of life? At age five, "Thou shalt not lie," carries meaning. This protective device, "I didn't do it. Johnny did it!!", can be used to escape possible punishment. Or at least it is worth a try. In another decade, "Thou shalt not steal," has real impact, as a teenager meets up with the prevelant "lark" of shop-lifting . . . "The others do it and get away with it!" Then add ten more years — "Thou shalt not commit adultery!" This can be a life-determining decision. Whether presented as "thou shalt not . . ." from God's Word, or just "situational ethics", *there stand those words — understanding and authority.*

Now let us consider that third ingredient — That one that ties it all together for us, as Christians. Outwardly, at least, we have acknowledged God as the original, final and rightful Authority and Judge. *Spiritual* authority — "Thus saith the Lord!" How has

God chosen to reveal and administer His authority? Remember we are not talking about ecclesiastical authority but *spiritual* authority. There is a difference.

THREE-DIMENSIONAL DISCLOSURE

Just as we have seen it in the physical realm, spiritual awareness has its definite origin, growth patterns and expectancies. To even *begin* to grasp God's plan and purpose in this area of His operation, we must recognize and accept some basic principles. One which we have previously shared is His three-pronged thrust for setting up authority in our present Church-age.

Recall Jesus' parable in Luke 20:9–16, as He tells about the Master of the vineyard sending his servants to collect the produce. The husbandmen disregard the delegated authority — beat the servants, and cast them out. They even went so far as to kill the son of the master when he was sent on his father's business. They reasoned they could claim the inheritance with him out of the way. Jesus then rasied the question: "What therefore shall the lord of the vineyard do unto them?" The answer came, "He shall come and destroy these husbandmen, and shall give the vineyard to others." Continued rejection of God's delegated authority results in finally rejecting God and going our own way — a rebel!

For an example of delegated authority, consider Paul and his words of greeting in Titus 1:1. "Paul a servant of God, and an apostle of Jesus Christ, *according to the faith of God's elect and the acknowledging of the truth which is after godliness.*"

To be operative, authority must be (1) *of* God . . . God had dramatically *called* Paul; (2) authority must be accepted by the one who is called by God . . . Paul had certainly gone all-out in his allegiance to his new-found Lord; and (3) that authority *must be accepted* by those to whom God's man is sent.

Do you remember those important words of Jesus in Matthew 23:29, "Blessed is he that comes in the name of the Lord." Again in Matthew 10:40, "He that receiveth you receiveth me, and he that receiveth me receiveth him that sent me." Do you see where God puts Himself in this matter? He stands just one step behind His delegated authority. How we treat His servants determines our measure of seeing, hearing and growing in spiritual truths. Permit me to share with you two stories which bring home this divine arrangement. One is from my own ministry and the other from the life of a friend.

I had just finished preaching my first Sunday night sermon. I felt it had been a miserable message and I had died a thousand deaths there behind the pulpit. Walking up the aisle to greet the people after it was over, a little old Polish lady approached me and said, "Brudder Mumford, can I pray for you?" She was trembling all over . . . inwardly, I was, too. Pray for me? God's man of faith and power who had come to straighten everybody out? A woman? But God said, "You had better submit." So I knelt down on a pew in front of where she was standing and bowed my head — I knew I was in need. As she laid her hands on my head, the power of God came upon me . . . from top to toes . . . fingertips and all! Mentally, I asked, "God, how come you gave that to this little old lady?" But the Lord had sent to me a servant and she came to me in the Name of the Lord.

My friend, an Episcopalian priest, lay in the hospital. He was in so much pain that about all he could do was cry out to God for relief. A critical spinal operation lay before him. Through his hospital doorway comes a casual acquaintance — a Pentecostal preacher — full of life and high spirits. He shouts, "Hello, Father! Jesus sent me to pray for you!" The noise shoots more pain up and down that spine. The very thought of enduring, even for a few moments, that boisterous contact is repungent. Coming closer, the visitor asks again, "Is it all right if I pray for you?" It seemed the easiest way out of an unhappy situation, so my friend nodded consent.

Relating the story to me, he said, "That man clamped his hands down on my head, pain mounting all the while. He bumped the bed and prayed loud enough to be heard all the way to heaven. He did everything wrong . . . and then he was gone. I almost thought I was, too! But as I lay there, I suddenly realized there was no more pain. It was such a relief and surprise that it took me quite some time to accept it." Simply · because God's servant was received, God's power was released.

Too often we want our ministry directly from God. We want personal attention. We aren't about to receive what we need through some delegated representative. It works the same way, not only in isolated instances of ministry, but in receiving teaching and new revelations of His desires for us. We are prone to say, "I get my orders straight from God." Remember, God doesn't come after the grapes Himself . . . He sends His servants. It is a three-way stretch which God has ordained. And God blesses or afflicts us with "servants" according to our needs.

STAND UNDER OR AGAINST

Turning to God's Word, Romans 13:1–5, look with me for a moment at the difference between power and authority. In verse one, the word *power* is used is some translations, but *authority* is the literal translation of the Greek word used here. Do you know the difference between the two? Authority is the badge that the policeman wears. Power is the gun he carries. If the badge doesn't get across the message, the gun will. Again, if a Greyhound bus is coming up the road, the officer doesn't stop the bus with power — he stops it with authority.

(1) "Let every soul (every person) *be subject (submit) unto the higher authorities. For there is no authority but of God; the authorities that be are ordained of God.*

(2) "Whosoever therefore resisteth the authority, resisteth the ordinance (command) *of God; and they that resist shall receive to themseves damnation* (the literal word is judgment; this is not going to hell — not at all).

(3) "For rulers are not a terror to good works, but to the evil. Wilt thou then not be afraid of the authority? do that which is good, and thou shalt have praise of the same;

(4) "For he is the minister of God to thee for good. But if thou do that which is evil, be afraid; for he beareth not the sword (his gun) *in vain: for he is the minister of God* (the one who fixes up those who have rebellion . . . Mumford's translation!) *a*

revenger to execute wrath upon him that doeth evil.

(5) "Wherefore ye must (it is necessary) *for you to be subject not only for wrath, but also for conscience sake."*

Two very important words are presented in these brief verses: *subject* and *resist*. Both are used not just once but several times. The literal translation of "subject" is two words and means "to stand under". The word "resist" is of the same Greek construction and means "to stand against". In any given situation you have only two choices — stand under or stand against! We must learn that when we feel this thing called resistance (or rebellion) rise up, we are obligated to recognize it and call it by its rightful name — *rebellion* — before it takes over. This means every soul — grandmother to child. Not a pleasant pill to swallow, is it? We might as well admit that it is not easy to submit and that even the word isn't palatable! But we can learn — and we must!

So . . . I come out from the grocery store and there is a ticket for overtime parking on my car. I want to rise up and stand against the whole police department. I tear up the ticket and three weeks later comes a knock at the door — it is the constable. I can resist him . . . and resist the judge . . . "It's unfair!" . . . . "Thirty days!" I can be in jail and have only one thought . . . "Just wait until I get out!"

We have two choices: stand under and let that rebel die — or stand against and watch that rebel grow. Do you know that there is nothing anybody can do with you if you really want to be a rebel? The police know this is true. Workers with children and youth know it. Is this happening in our day? We have a whole generation that is standing against authority . . . parental . . . governmental . . . spiritual. As this evil element spreads, the feeling permeates into the church. The whole world may be going one way, but God asks the Church to go His way.

Verse 2 tells us, "They that stand against, shall receive to themselves judgment." It does not say that it is God who is judging me. When I stand against, I am judging myself a rebel! As I continue in my rebellion, I become blind — not just to the facts inherent in a given situation, or against people involved — but I become blinded to the things of God. God has built His kingdom structure in such a way that it automatically excludes all rebels. You rebel . . . darkness grows; and you receive to yourself judgment. God does not judge. Oh, no. You do it yourselves. Listen, when you feel resistance rise in you, break. Stand under it! It is not for the sake of the authorities — whether they are right or wrong — the thing is this: God is giving you an opportunity to break that core of rebellion that is buried in your spirit. If that breaks, everything else will fall into place.

God has His laws. We stand or fall according to our choices. It involves individual responsibility. One day the Lord said to me: "Mumford, you and I are imcompatible, and I don't change." It took awhile for that statement to sink in. Have you felt the full force of that truth yet? Most of us know how to manipulate and maneuver our parents and others who cross our paths. We know how to get our own way. This makes me doubly thankful that God cannot be bought . . . He cannot be threatened . . . He will never be out-maneuvered. There is no escape. You avoid Him at one turn along the road and later you will meet up with Him around the next bend. He's there waiting!

FEARS/PROBLEMS/ANSWERS

Rising up out of this divine arrangement of delegated authority come some fears and problems. As we take our expected stand under the authority God has placed immediately over us, question marks appear on the horizon. But God has provided the answers and they are available to the honest seeker.

Two fears in the Body of Christ are (1) that there will be no authority, and (2) that there will be wrong authority. Some of us are even afraid of the word "authority". Consequently, there are spiritual Lone Rangers. These ride off by themselves and admit to no need of anyone. "Just me and God." From my observation, it is mighty rough going out there riding the range all alone. It puts the fear of God in many of us because we realize that where there is no authority, the wolves have free access. Also, there is the danger of falling into the plight recorded in Judges 17:6: "In those days there was no king in Israel, *but every man did that which was right in his own eyes.*"

Then the fear of wrong authority: pitfalls here, too. We hesitate to submit for fear the one under whom we take our stand may ask us to do something we feel we just do not want to do! A strong plea from a mission field may come and the cry go out, "Everybody empty your bank accounts and give it to missions!" Is this a basic distrust of God?

Two problems add themselves for consideration:

(1) that no one will want to submit; (2) that there will be spiritual dictators. Very real problems but with answers. As the Church moves into obedience, the listening ones will willingly come into subjection to the authority God places over them. And God will increasingly raise up men to places of authority who, in turn, will be submissive, themselves, and thus prove capable leadership.

Speaking of spiritual dictators, much criticism has been leveled in the past (and some of it justifiable) against ecclesiastical hierarchy and authority. But if we take a good square look at some of our smaller circles of operation, similar tendencies (only on a reduced scale) might be brought to light . . . and that not of choice but perhaps necessity!

Often some of the fears and problems we rasie prove to be only smoke-screens behind which we hope to take refuge. I believe God is moving throughout the entire Body in an effort to open our eyes to His ways and means platforms. The Holy Spirit is bringing us into the whole truth in order to set us free — not to bring us into bondage, as some would have us believe. Jesus tells of this coming facet of the Spirit's work in John 16:13, "Howbeit when he, the Spirit of truth, is come, he will guide you into *all truth* . . ." Authority needs to be received to become effective.

As to the possibility of authority being misrepresented, God can take care of this aspect, too. We must admit that once some of us taste the power of having authority over others, basic conflicts can arise. This is demonstrated in the following father-son situation.

My two boys engage in some back-and-forth

argument. The older one finally gets tired of it and comes to me with the complaint, "Daddy, I can't do anything with my brother."

Asserting my parental authority, I say: "Well, go back in there and tell him, Daddy said . . ."

Willing to give it a try, I hear: "You had better get in bed. Daddy said so." It worked! Do you see how easy it would be to put that magical phrase in use to one's own advantage? "Daddy says do this . . . Daddy says don't do that . . ." And all the time Daddy may be unaware of misuse of his authority. But God is never "otherwise occupied" . . . or out of town . . . or caught off guard. He can protect and retract His authority!

We can use this same technique not only to brandish a club over those in submission to us, but, also, to worm our way out of submitting to someone. It is easy to say, *"God told me . . ."* when we want to go or get our own way. Nobody can argue with that, because He *is* the highest authority there is. If each one of us will stand guard over his own proper use of authoratative prerogatives, we will have less time to be questioning that of others.

How about this statement for a scorcher? *A rebel seeks to find fault with the authority over him so he will not have to submit!* "I don't like purple ties . . . his hair is too long . . . preachers shouldn't dirve Cadillacs . . ." Some "people-watchers" are constantly on the alert for any and all reasons for non-submission. As far as they are concerned, they have never yet met anybody good enough to warrant their submission and they have a little hard-core of rebellion to prove it. They might as well come right out and admit that what they really are after is to go their own way . . . run their own lives . . . do their "own thing" — irrespective and unbridled!

UNDER-COVER AGENTS

And we might as well "tell it like it is" and try to hear it like it's told! To be effective kingdom agents, with proper working credentials, we all must be *under cover.* That goes for everyone — stem to stern. Paul recognized this principle and presented it in no uncertain terms. In Ephesians 5:21, he states: "Submitting (standing under) yourselves one to another in the fear of God." Then he goes on and speaks specifically to wives, hsubands, children, servants, masters. In 6:10, he wraps it up, "Finally, my brethren, be strong in the Lord, and in the power of his might." Then comes the admonition to put on the whole armor of God, closing with a request for prayer, . . . "And for me, *that utterance may be given unto me, that I may open my mouth boldly, to make known the mystery of the Gospel.*"

This is just what I want to do here and now — share with you what I have been learning about "covering". What may seem new to us, proves to have been available to us all the time. In order to "spell it out", let's begin by saying that God establishes authority in the earth. He puts someone directly over each area of His creation. On the sixth day of His creative activities, He spoke to Adam and Eve: ". . . and replenish the earth, and subdue it: and have dominion over the fish of the sea, and over the fowl of the air, and over every living thing that moveth upon the earth." *All* should have someone over them, in the Lord, to whom they answer. This is submission — "Let every soul stand under."

The home was the first God-ordained unit of society. The husband/father was placed at the head of the home. Most of us men have assumed a position of "male" leadership in our homes — handy to have around when the furniture needs moving and such related "strong man" responsibilities — but we are speaking of *spiritual headship*.

One of the wide-spread depictions in the area of home-life in our entertainment world today is the movie and television portrayals — along with the comic strip characters — showing "dear old dad" as a bumbling, stumbling idiot who trips over the coffee table, with the wife and children helpfully guiding him along through life. There is also a profusion of husbands without wives, and wives without husbands, who are all trying to make it on their own. This affords a lot of laughs along the road . . . but when the surface is scratched, the pathos shows through. Male mediocrity and female liberation are two sides of the coin that Satan is trying to pawn off on us today. Church, hear me, don't buy it!

In the Mumford household there have been some adjustments, just as there are in every home. Picture things as they ought to be: father, priest of the home . . . in his proper place over his family — a spiritual covering. *This is as they ought to be!* The following "before and after" presentation depicts part of our "transition".

SCENE I (Some years before we really began to understand what was going on): Father goes off on an extended teaching mission. My wife, two daughters and two sons are left at the mercy of the devil. Sure enough . . . things begin to go wrong. The refrigerator stops working. The car won't start. Children are wanting to run off in all directions. Sickness . . . confusion . . . questions! My wife, Judy, gets on the phone: "Honey, you just have to come home . . ."

Here am I away trying to do the will of God! I had a hard time figuring it all out. Then I saw two things. First, I was not taking my rightful place as the priest in my home. When the priest is not taking his place, as ordained of God, the home is uncovered and demon activity comes in and out at will, causing havoc. The home and family are under attack. Secondly, when I take my stand and assert it in the home, that home is under covering. I said, "Devil, listen to me. This home belongs to Jesus Christ. I am priest of this home and you get your hands off!" What happened?

Scene II Father is off again on a trip . . . the phone calls take on a different tone. I call, "How are things going, honey?" Answer: "Great . . .We miss you . . . praying for you . . ." I began to see the covering of the Lord come down over my whole home — financially, physically and spiritually. God healed and helped in every area.

But, if my wife rejects my ministry, I am in trouble. If my wife receives my ministry, she receives from me. The same goes for the children. This is *covering.*

What about persons who are not in a "home" situation — the singles, the widows, the divorced? I often wondered why God commanded His people to . . ."take care of the widows, visit the fatherless." Now I am beginning to understand this was not just to make sure they had money and food in the house.

God was calling on the men in the leadership of the church to take care of these who had no covering, that they might be protected, not just from the physical demands of their aloneness, but from the rebellion that can result from having to stand unprotected in the spiritual realm. No one is made that way. We need each other.

This principle is valid in a prayer group . . . a church . . . and it also applies to men in individual ministries. When God said, "let every soul be subject . . .", He meant just what He said. When I am called to a certain area to teach, I go first to my brothers to whom I am submitted in Fort Lauderdale. After prayer and laying on of hands, I feel that I go out to serve with the blessing of God upon my ministry. I go as a submitted member of the Body of Christ. Frankly, it was not always like that. But God said, "Mumford . . . Oh, Mumford . . ." I began the ". . . but, Lord . . ." response. He would have none of it! We are all in the learning stages and the Master Teacher knows just how to bring us around.

What if your particular "covering" doesn't come up to your plans and specifications? Is this any excuse to "come out from under"? No. Your responsibility is to take that one to the Lord. You may be certain that once you have taken your proper place, God is going to test you. The rain may come through a few holes in the roof, but ask God to patch up the leaks.

Wife, you may feel you know more scripture verses than your husband . . . you listen to more tapes . . . but . . .

Teen-ager, you may feel Dad has been a bit rough on you and you are going to stay out all night to prove to him you are entitled to a few rights of your own, but . . .

Church member, you may not like the color the pastor has chosen for the new carpet in the sanctuary — and you . . . chairman of the committee for raising funds . . . but . . .

Do you know how to tell the difference between the sheep and the goats? Sheep don't butt! Is that excuse you make a cover-up for your rebellious spirit? The "buts" are not an acceptable reason for your lack of submission.

When you come into submission, this is when your rebellion will be revealed, should any be lurking in dark corners hoping to avoid exposure. This affords God the opportunity to present to you the privilege of making changes and adjustments in that attitude. I have had my own children pray me into a place of submission. With submission, comes a wonderful release. The driving spirit that often keeps us going full steam ahead, churning up a heat of religious fervancy that is really only froth, subsides and we settle down into a spiritual maturity that brings cleansing and joy.

To experience the outworking of this principle, each one must search out and find someone to whom he can *verbally* submit.

Children go to your parents and *tell* them, "Dad . . . Mom . . . I have been rebellious. But I wan to submit to you." Do the same to your school teacher.

Wives, make it clear to your husbands, in *words*, that your wish is to take your stand under his covering.

Every minister . . . missionary . . . worker in the

kingdom must have someone to whom he is submitted.

Remember, once you submit, then comes the test to see if you said it only with your mouth — or if you meant it from your heart. Also, remember when the test comes, the one thing that determines whether you pass or fail is your determination to maintain your stand and relate in a submissive attitude, even if you do not agree in every situation. I know of a church where the members took the stand that "our" pastor is right, even when he is wrong. God has blessed this church financially, spiritually and every other way. One can feel the presence of God when he goes into that gathering.

Yes, God is moving us into new territory — and there are some dangers. However, no danger in exploring and claiming new territory is as hazardous as the danger of continuing in rebellion. Submission breaks that core of rebellion and as it breaks we are set free. We are brought into a new spiritual relationship whereby we stand under one another, as well as standing beside each other. Continual confusion subsides and in its place comes the fulfillment of Jesus' prayer to His Father:

"That they may all be one; as thou, Father, art in me, and I in thee, that they also may be one in us; that the world may believe that thou hast sent me." (John 17:21)

Chapter Five

THE NATURE OF OBEDIENCE

Twentieth Century inventions! What a Pandora's box that thought opens. No flight of imagination too high . . . no degradation too low . . . no field too wide . . . nothing too microscopic. Descriptions like instant, automatic, quickie — these are labels which we accept and investigate every day. The "instants" range from mashed potatoes to the replay of a sporting event detail we might have missed by the blink of an eye. The "automatics" are found in very area of our daily life. The automatic vending machine alone dispenses a more varied line than F.W. Woolworth and Heinz ever dreamed up. And the "quickies" cover the complex and the simple — divorce to dress pattern; take your pick! No doubt about it, the U.S. Bureau of Patents is big business.

With all this display of originality and creativity, how does it happen that God — the Author of both — comes up with a strange mechanism that still operates on the same old formula that it always has? *Obedience,* the strange mechanism in question, doesn't come neatly packaged with any of the above labels attached. God designed that particular commodity and He owns the copyright.

So, God didn't arrange for obedience to be instant. Some people labor under the misconception that one day a ball of fire or an earthquake will appear over the horizon. As a result they will be endued from on high with either an outer protection that will turn away all the fiery darts of temptation — or an inner thermostat will be installed and set at a certain temperature . . . then . . . no more worries!

Neither did God design obedience to be automatic. No four dreams . . . three visions . . . two angels are going to get the job done. That is, unless one of the angels appears with a board in his hand. That might accomplish the purpose for awhile.

As for the quickies, nothing here. Obedience cannot be boiled down to a single recipe: add a little of this, a dash of that, so much fasting, certain amount of prayer — blend well, place in the oven of adversity for such and such a length of time — end result, *OBEDIENCE* — guaranteed results every time.

PRINCIPLES

Our purpose in this study is to establish principles, not methods. First, how do we know if we are obedient or disobedient?

Take Johnny for example. At age three, he is mother's little darling. The two of them meet a friend in the drug store. The friend exclaims over Johnny's marked growth since last they met. Kind words bring out the mother-desire to display her son's sweet disposition. "Smile for the kind lady, Johnny." Scowl from Johnny. "Honey, smile for the lady." Second request comes through gritted teeth. More scowl! You see, Johnny was so nice until he was given a command.

When one of my daughters was about Johnny's age, the two of us had a similar go-round. She had put a block up on her mother's knick-knack shelf. I tried to get across to her that I wanted her to remove the block . . . that it did not belong on the shelf. After several attempts at, "Honey, take the block off the shelf," with no results, I decided she did not know what I meant. I took her little hand and placed it on the block with the same request. Still no response. It began to dawn on me that she was quite aware of my desire and equally certain of hers. So I initiated another line of attack, which brought howls and a definite, "No!!" Rebellion at age three? I might add that about forty-five minutes later she removed the block.

Commandments are specific instructions. They are given by someone who has authority and are expected to be obeyed. People often are afraid of the very word, *commandment,* saying we are no longer under the law . . . bondage will result . . . legalism lurks within these confines. Something we need to understand is that God always expected us to keep His commandments. It is not whether we should or should not keep them — but *how* we keep them. The spirit in which we accept and obey is all-important.

The word *commandment* is used seventy one times in the New Testament and someone has estimated there are over one thousand commandments in those same twenty-seven books of the Bible. Does this convey something of what we are driving at?

In order to know the will of God, we must search out His commandments. By carefully measuring our responses to them, we can guage the extent of our obedience. For example:

"If ye love me, keep my commandments. . ." John 13:21.

''*He   that   breaks   one   of   these*

commandments . . ." Matthew 22:4.

". . . be mindful of the commandments which we gave you." II Peter 3:2.

"Circumcision is nothing . . . but the keeping of the commandments of God." I Corinthians 7:9.

"If we say that we love Him and keep not His commandments . . ." I John 2:4.

''Blessed are they that do his commandments . . ." Revelation 22:14.

Doesn't this sound as if the Lord were putting the burden upon us? The truth is, that He is!

PROCEDURES

Taking a passage from the Old Testament — Isaiah 50:4—7 — let us investigate some aspects of obedience:

(4) "The Lord God hath given me the tongue of the learned, that I should know how to speak a word in season to him that is weary; he wakeneth morning by morning, he wakeneth mine ear to hear as the learned.

(5) "The Lord God hath opened mine ear, and I was not rebellious, neither turned away back.

(6) "I gave my back to the smiters, and my cheeks to them that plucked off the hair: I hid not my face from shame and spitting.

(7) "For the Lord God will help me; therefore shall I not be confounded: therefore have I set my face like a flint, and I know that I shall not be ashamed."

Included in these verses is a most moving prophetic word about the obedience of our Lord Jesus Christ. How did He learn this valuable lesson? Hebrews 5:8

gives the answer: "Though he were a son, yet learned he obedience by the things which he suffered." Suffering? Not a very enticing type of training program, is it?

Wouldn't it be wonderful if obedience could be secured as a gift? If I, or anyone else, could impart this precious ability, a line would form from here to "kingdom come" wanting to receive this particular ministry. Why not, once for all, acknowledge and accept the fact that God, Maker of heaven and earth, *made obedience a learned accomplishment*.

Returning to Isaiah, notice the first three words, "The Lord God". Here is the Teacher. This very fact should draw us into the classroom, even if that obejctionable notation, "suffering", is written over the doorway.

Next, look at the following phrase, "hath given me", Yes, there is a reward for those enrolling. Using good advertising technique, we find the results well displayed. Many ads tell of the results that may be expected by those accepting a certain opportunity to learn. However, "Sit down at the piano and hold your audience spellbound," doesn't promise that this will happen the *first time* you sit down at the paino! God *does* promise results. "He hath given me the tongue of the learned, that I should *know how . . .*" Know-how! This is a common aim in every sphere of education.

Here comes another proven procedure: "morning by morning". Every skill is acquired this way — REPITITION. Conquering proper control of a piano . . . a typewriter . . . an automobile, takes constant "doing". God has ordained that we learn obedience this same way — day by day. Yesterday and tomorrow are not on His agenda. It is a TODAY thing.

TODAY you have the opportunity to obey the Lord. What you aim to do tomorrow does not count. Do the words, "Take up your cross daily" (Jesus speaking), sound familiar?

If we are honestly seeking an answer to the obedient/disobedient question, we have been given a safeguard. Each night as I place my head upon the pillow in preparation for sleep, I can ask, "Did I obey TODAY?" God has providentially placed nights between days, not only for restoral of physical fitness, but also as a restoral of the spiritual. We can admit failure if we must. We can ask forgiveness and accept it, taking our night's rest assured that the new day will bring fresh opportunities to obey. Or, if we feel we have been obedient, we can offer praise and thanksgiving for a day in which we have known the joy of pleasing our Father.

Strange as it may seem to us, we can go from week to week, month to month, even from year to year without taking advantage of this nightly inventory. But as we prolong the desire to check our obedience, obedience itself fades away into self-determined standards for our actions.

Looking over "instruction sheet", we note this: "He wakeneth mine ear . . . He opened mine ear." The literal Hebrews reads, "The Lord God hath digged mine ear." The ability to hear in such a way as to respond as the one speaking desires, is not "natural". It must be learned. We usually hear what we want to hear. But with God "digging" my ear, I become trained to recognize His voice and anticipate His desires. When I do not *want* to hear, I have the ability to "turn it off". This is much the same action we exert when we turn off a certain television or radio program. We can blank out our receptive powers to receive God's Word, His voice, His commands, His servants. Jesus spoke of ". . . having ears, hear ye not?" (Mark 8:18).

Look with me at some verses that bring out the fact that the word *obey* means to "hear under" — or to hear in such a way that there is a response . . . hear and submit!

"But the men marvelled, saying, What manner of man is this, that even the winds and sea obey him." Matthew 8:27.

"And they were all amazed, insomuch that they questioned among themselves, saying, What is this? What new doctrine is this? for with authority commandeth he even the unclean spirits, and they do obey him." Mark 1:27.

"Seeing ye have purified your souls in obeying the truth through the Spirit." I Peter 1:22.

One last look at our selection from Isaiah: ". . . and I was not rebellious." Here is the key. In the final analysis, the responsibility is ours. The lessons may be perfectly planned and outlined — the teacher may be the most capable — and yet the student may fail completely! *I was not rebellious.* Morning by morning we can say, "Lord dig my ear to hear — and grant me an obedient spirit that I may respond."

PROVISIONS

God has instituted two avenues along which we may learn obedience. Active and passive. Do you recall our illustration about the training necessary for preparing dogs for police duty? Fido had to become equally acquainted with two commands: "Fetch" as well as, "Heel!" After racing off to retrieve and return the object the officer had thrown into the field, trying to sit at attention and watch that object beckoning to him, required real effort. So it is with us. God has provided the means whereby we can "hear under" Him commands like: "Go and do . . . say . . . give." We also receive another type of command: "Sit down and keep quiet . . . stop . . . wait . . . come apart before you come apart."

The first set of orders involves active participation as He works through us. The second involves submitting while He works on us. These latter may be situations that are difficult to understand, and I may find myself wanting to get out of them. *Learning is a process that has to be embraced voluntarily. You learn to obey!*

Let me share with you another wonderful provision that God has made in this classroom. He not only furnishes the desire to obey, but He also provides the means through which we can fulfill this desire.

In understanding the nature and character of obedience, we must realize that nature is given — character is developed. The first is innate, the second is acquired. When we were born again, we received a new nature — His nature. Innate in that nature was a tremendous longing to obey and please God. But the "how-to" is another matter. *The desire to obey is not obedience.* For an example, we take Jesus. We mentioned briefly before that although He was the sinless Son of God, He learned obedience by the things He suffered . . . Hebrews 5:

(7) "Who in the days of His flesh, when he had offered up prayers and supplications with strong cryings and tears unto him that was able to save him from death, was heard in that he feared:

(8) "Though he were a Son, yet learned he obedience by the things which he suffered:

(9) "And being made perfect, he became the author of eternal salvation unto all them that obey him."

Jesus had a sinless nature. Inside was the desire to do His father's will. But doing that will required that He obey, just as it does of us. Every time Jesus had a chance to obey, He was obedient. Jesus said, "I only do that which My Father tells me to do." It happened along a dusty road in Galilee as He met the needs of a blind beggar. "Son, mix a little spit and mud . . ." It also happened when He heard His Father say, "Son, it is now time to go up to Jerusalem." And He set His face like a flint, heading toward Jerusalem. Here we see Him on the avenue of active obedience.

Then look as, "I gave my back to the smiters . . . and my cheeks to them that plucked off the hair . . . I hid not my face from shame and spitting." Our second avenue, that of passive obedience, had some hours of agony. However, the life of our Lord Jesus can be reduced to this; His ability to hear and to respond. He could truly say, "I only do that which my Father tells me to do." Obedience was worked in the Son by the Father — day by day.

Returning to an experience many of us have shared, let me relate my battle with the typewriter. This came as an assignment given me when I was in the Navy. As I punched that typewriter, I complained, "How can you learn to type when they give you a keyboard with no letters on it? That's the dumbest thing I ever saw." All the while I was beating on that machine and it kept right on misspelling. With "strong crying and tears", I persevered. Suddenly that thing began to click . . . click . . . click, and to my amazement — it started spelling!

So you learn . . . you miss it . . . you hit it. Morning by morning, you keep at it. Soon you begin to understand and respond. An early command from Him may be, "Put your Tastee-Freeze quarter in the offering today." You obey and twenty years later, He may ask for $1000 for a specific need. Because you gave that quarter, you are able to hear and heed His request in later years. Some, however, are still clutching quarters and missing blessings.

PROBLEMS

How far dare we go in this matter of obedience? Dare I "come under authority" and obey, thereby laying myself open to demands I may not care to obey? There are hazards, but let me tell you this: from my experience, I have found that the one who dared to obey is the one who comes out right in the end.

One hurdle along the way is that of being over-zealous. The danger here is that the Enemy may come in, take advantage of us, and we will mis-apply our desire to obey. Satan is always on the alert for an opening in the door into which he can stick his big foot, hoping for entrance and control. He would be mighty stupid if he didn't give it a try. This possibility of mis-direction needs careful consideration.

When I came back to God after twelve years of "doing my own thing", I came back 208%. "Others can play games, but I am going to press in . . . I am going to be spiritual at all costs!" Talk about the devil's delight! He began to give me all kinds of leadings and calls and directions. One day my wife said, "Honey, it really puzzles me that God would call a man to go in eight directions at the same time." When I stopped long enough to think about it, I had to admit that it didn't sound reasonable. Who called me to go eight directions at once? Your guess is as good as mine was. Satan knew that by keeping me going full-steam, multi-divided, self-directed, I would soon become ineffective . . . scattered . . . and, eventually, I would destroy myself, my family and my ministry.

Let me say something that may prove helpful right here. We need to realize that submission is total; obedience is relative. Insubordination is always wrong; but I can have a submitted attitude without obeying in every instance. Submission is an attitude; obedience is conduct. Does this have a familiar ring? We emphasized in our consideration of Lawlessness, that rebellion is an attitude — and sin is conduct. Two events in the life of the early church brings this into focus.

In Acts, Chapter 5, we read the account of the arrest of the apostles by Jewish authorities for teaching and preaching Jesus. The high priest reminded the prisoners that they had already been commanded not to preach in "this name". Peter's response was: "We ought to obey God rather than men." Here is displayed a submissive attitude, yet a firm stand on what he considered right in this particular situation. Peter could have said, "You're not going to tell us what to do. We are the holy ones, anointed of God. We don't obey anybody but Him!"

The result of Peter's submissive attitude before the council is evident in Gamaliel's decision: ". . . refrain from these men, and let them alone: for if this counsel of this work be of men, it will come to nought. But if it be of God, ye cannot overthrow it; lest haply ye be found even to fight against God . . . And they agreed." The incident ended without further argument. Had Peter assumed a defiant attitude, the hearing could have been the beginning of an uprising.

Further in the Book of Acts (Chapter 23) we find Paul before a Jewish council and on much the same type of charge. Paul made a remark in verse one which was interpreted by the high priest as insubordination. The order was given to strike Paul across the face. Hear Paul as he explains, "I wist not, brethren, that he was the high priest: for it is written, Thou shalt not speak evil of the ruler of thy people."

Do you see that as Paul chose the route of submission that he was actually "standing under" authority? This position is the one that breaks any rebellion that might still be trying to manifest itself. Paul, Peter, John — all of these men faced the problems of rebellion and obedience just as we do. And they solved their problems in exactly the same way in which we must tackle ours.

All right, we have established the fact that *submission is total and absolute — obedience is relative.* We have three guides to help us make our

decisions as "when to" . . . "how far" . . . "Why
not". First and foremost is the Word of God. Second
is the voice of God (the ministry of the Holy Spirit).
The third is the authority that God has placed over
us. Never forget which is first. Both the voice and the
authority are measured by the Word of God.

Then there are three areas where authority is
exerted: the spiritual realm (this would include
pastors, elders, prayer group leaders); the home
(husbands, wives, parents); and our civil authorities.
The question we must ask ourselves as we decide
what to do about commands in these three areas is —
Is it illegal . . . immoral . . . unscriptural? We can
and should be able to assume a submitted attitude
and say, "I submit to you up this this point, but I
cannot do what you are asking me to do."

However, the shoe may be put on the other foot,
and we can end up refusing to submit, not because
the request involves anything immoral, unscriptural
or illegal, but because of rebellion on our part.

In a certain family, parents may feel it necessary to
say, "Mary, you are going to 27 prayer meetings a
week. We feel, for the benefit of your
school-work . . . your health . . . things here at
home, you should choose five of these meetings and
drop off the other twenty-two." Instantly the cry
goes up, "My parents won't let me be a Christian.
They are trying to prevent me from walking with
God." Any rebel in that reply?

Let me ask, too, is there a difference between a
husband asking his wife to go fishing with him and
accompanying him to a pornographic movie? Yes.
But there is no need to get super-spiritual in
considering either request.

A wife may feel, in regard to the first request, that she would much prefer to stay home and read or study. Fishing may seem a complete waste of time to her. But Peter warned, "Wives, fit in to your husband's plans." (Literal translation of I Peter 3:1). By acquiescing, even though putting worms on a hook and taking sticky fish off the hook are not the wife's idea of "fun", she can find true joy in standing in that boat and saying, "Lord, I want you to know that there is nobody else in the world that I would do this for but you."

As to the second request, a wife can, by her very attitude, set the stage as she says: "Joe, you know I love you and I am your submitted wife. But, irrespective of all this, I cannot go to that movie." Very few people "in authority" will take advantage of a genuinely submissive attitude. Some, perhaps, but very few.

Agreed, each of us had a right to "draw the line". Also, each one is held responsible for setting that line as far away from any tendency toward rebellion as possible. There is no scriptural command, "Thou shalt not go fishing", but there is one that says, "Abstain from evil." Guard against permitting a rebellious spirit drawing the line. Thus you will learn to hear God's directions in all decisions.

PROMISES

Jesus said, "He that hath ears to hear, let him hear . . ." (Matthew 11:15). What did He mean? We have all been given ears as standard equipment. Why is it that some hear and others do not? We are speaking of spiritual impairment, not physical. The answer, in a single word, is that word we have placed before us, *Obedience.*

When God speaks to us of His love and His desire to restore us to a right relationship to Himself as our Father, we have the choice of accepting or refusing that offer. Once we accept and become a memeber of His family, we are automatically enroled in the School of Obedience. We are given an ability to hear, along with our new nature which contains a desire to obey. From that moment on, we *can* hear His voice, *if we want to.* His Word is placed at our disposal for instruction; His Spirit is made available for fellowship and guidance; and authority is always present, as no one is exempt from earthly rule.

We can soon become so sensitive to God's commands that our ears will pick up His slightest whisper. Just as a mother adjusts her hearing to catch in her infant's cry what his needs are, we can catch in every circumstance in life, His Presence. Just as a doctor listens to his patients as they discuss symptoms, all the while diagnosing the cause of the trouble, we can gain an understanding of causes and cures within ourselves.

On the other side of the hearing question, we can so insensitize our hearing apparatus that "it goes in one ear and out the other". One day I was in an office where on the outside a building was being erected . . . pilings were being driven . . . the noise was deafening. I asked the receptionist, "How do you stand that noise out there?" Her nonchalant reply was, "What noise?" A condition like this might be called, "thickening of the ear drum"! Isn't it wonderful how nature adjusts itself to its environment? There is also an adjustment that adjusts itself in spiritual perception. When we "turn down our hearing aid" as God speaks, through His Word, His Spirit, or delegated authority, the same result is evidenced . . . "What commands?"

Man's Twentieth Century invention of a streamlined, atom-operated hearing aid restores to many the joy of hearing. But God is not depending on man's ingenuity in the spiritual realm. There is no substitute or supplement for obedience.

Constant refusal to obey His commands will so harden our ear-drums that we become unable to hear what He is saying . . . to see what He is doing . . . and, eventually, it can close our spirit to His entrance. We labeled this final result of harboring a rebellious spirit, *The Great Transgression,* about which David warned us in Psalm 19:13.

May God help us to realize that no invention of man can ever supersede or replace the originally ordained plans of the Creator. May He help us, too, as we seek to understand and accept these plans.

Chapter Six

THE SPIRIT OF OBEDIENCE
OR LEARNING TO OBEY

Once, while conducting a teaching seminar, I became concerned about how much the seminarians were "receiving". Presenting my problem to the Lord, I suggested, "God, I surely would like to give these students an exam." To which came the instant reply, "You do the teaching. I will give the examination!" You can be certain that He did just that; and you can be equally certain that He will be examining each of us who has shared in these teachings on OBEDIENCE.

In order to prepare ourselves for this eventuality, here are some observations for review. Remember — the Word of God is seed — and the teaching of it is expected to bring forth growth. Will it be ten-fold? sixty-fold? Or a hundred . . . straight A?

LAWLESSNESS is a spirit; it invades and infects Christians as well as those "of the world".

THE GREAT TRANSGRESSION is rebellion; it is an attitude which rises up within a person (1) under the circumstances of life (2) under the dealings of God.

COMMANDMENTS are specific instructions — given by someone in authority — and obedience is expected.

SUBMIT OR RESIST? Here is individual choice. The one who resists, judges himself "rebel".

A REBEL seeks to find fault with the authority over him so that he will have an excuse for not submitting.

THE SPIRIT in which a person accepts and obeys authority is extremely important.

GOD REVEALS our measure of rebellion by putting authority over us — be it piano teacher . . . parent . . . pastor . . .

OBEDIENCE is not automatic; it is a learned accomplishment. Also, the desire to obey is NOT obedience.

DELEGATED AUTHORITY, civil or spiritual, stands as a question mark in the test of rebellion.

GOD BLESSES OR AFFLICTS us with "delegated authority" according to our needs.

We move from the review of foundational facts into the loftiest realm of obedience — the realm of the unenforceable. It is in this stratosphere that man finds the deepest joys of fellowship with God. Here is the beautiful relationship of which Jesus spoke in John 15, 16 and 17 . . . we are one with Him and with the Father.

THE UNENFORCEABLES

Perhaps a family illustration may help us to grasp something of that which is involved in this word "unenforceable", as applied to obedience.

For weeks our family had been planning a vacation. We had looked forward to a long leisurely drive through new-to-us territory. Pleasure stops had been carefully marked on the roadmaps. Anticipation ran high. But as the time of departure drew near, the many details needing attention mounted almost to the point of erasing expectations. As we prepared for our early morning take-off, carefully checking for last minute slip-ups, we found ourselves short-tempered and almost too exhausted to realize that we were at last on our way. Hoping to arouse interest, I got behind the wheel of the car and exclaimed in a somewhat angry tone of voice, "All right everybody! Now we are going on vacation. Start having a good time!!!" Talk about a ton of bricks!

Or take the matter of love. Try saying, "You love me, or else . . ." We all know that one cannot threaten or coerce love. You cannot buy it. You can't do anything — love will not be forced. Remember, God Himself cannot make enforceable laws in certain realms. He can reveal principles but He cannot force obedience. *The spirit of obedience is when men obey in realms that are unenforceable.*

Most of us are familiar with the story of the child who was asked . . . then ordered . . . to sit down in his high chair before he fell out. Finally reluctantly complying, he retorted, "But I'm still standing up on the inside." We have all experienced at some time, in some situation, this outward compliance . . . coupled with inward resistance. We are aware of the necessity of having a desire . . . a will . . . an attitude that makes obedience really obedience in the highest sense of the word. This is what God is seeking in His children.

There is the legalistic approach to obedience, too. Recall the statement of the "certain ruler" who came to Jesus asking what he needed to do to inherit eternal life. He made it clear to Jesus that he had kept all the commandments from his youth up. And Jesus made it equally clear that there was one thing yet

The Spirit of Obedience or Learning to Obey   105

lacking (Luke 18:18-24). This one "thing" was in the realm of the unenforceable — giving and living as Jesus gave and lived — "sell what you have . . . give to the poor . . . and come and follow Me."

While I was in the pastorate, a legalistic spirit was visible in giving patterns. When the giving of a tithe was recorded "to the penny" — $10.02 when the income was $100.20 — the tendency to please God by keeping laws was evident. Anybody who walks *only* by laws is in trouble. Nobody can keep a person from lusting — even though he does not commit adultery. Nobody can keep one from being angry — even though "thou shalt not kill" is maintained. And putting priority on exact obedience to the letter of the law can never be a substitute for the spirit God desires from us. We cannot please God by keeping laws. We may please ourselves and present a good front to society, but this produces death to the spirit which God is trying to cultivate within us.

There was something within the heart of Jesus that can be ours, too. He wanted to do the will of the Father . . . He desired to do it in every circumstance of life.

I wish I could say this was always true with me. There are times when it has been a joy — especially in a meeting when the Spirit of God is moving. But get me out alone when nobody is around . . . the pressures are on . . . then it is a little more difficult! The achievement of this spirit of obedience is a work of the Holy Spirit. God said, "The day will come when I will write my laws on your heart" (Hebrews 8:10). This is a spiritual experience.

REALMS WITHOUT RULES

Are you willing to join me as we plunge down into the realm of the internal — this realm which bears the placard, "By Invitation Only"? No one — not even God can gain entrance here. Man is made a free moral agent. He has been given the privilege of opening the door to the workings of the Spirit — or he can keep it closed. With privilege always comes responsibility.

Let me share two verses of Scripture which envelope the invitation necessary to permit God to enter this inner realm and begin to do His work. Careful now . . . do not pray these petitions unless you are willing for Him not only to enter but to take up residence! For He must not only be present but be given free rein in order to accomplish His desired purpose.

"Let the words of my mouth and the meditations of my heart be acceptable in thy sight, O Lord, my strength and my redeemer" (Psalm 19:14).

"Search me, O God, and know the inward condition of my heart: try me (put someone over me, Lord, and I will show you how submitted I am) *and know my thoughts: And see if there be any wicked way in me, and lead me in the way everlasting" (Psalm 139:23,24).*

Are you beginning to catch the implications involved in accepting the fact that obedience is an attitude . . . that it is not primarily a matter of conduct? Do you see that God is not satisfied with merely the external keeping of commandments?

Direct acts of obedience are not intuitive. When we are born again, regenerated by the Holy Spirit, we are given a desire to obey. Yet there is quite a difference between the desire to do God's will and the ability to do it. But once that desire is resident, it is God's purpose to bring to us the ability to do His will.

Would you agree with me that there have been times in your life when you wanted to do somethings but did not know how to go about it? There have been times when I have wanted to be a good father and I didn't know how. There have been times when I have wanted to be a good husband and didn't know how. There have also been times when I wanted to be a carpenter and I cut the board off three times and it was still too short! I wanted to do things but I just did not know how to do them.

Taking one phrase from Psalm 19:14, let's look at one realm where the inner spirit of man is revealed: "the words of my mouth." Jesus once said, ". . . of the abundance of the heart the mouth speaketh" (Luke 6:45b). How much damage has been done by "the words of my mouth"!! Three areas where we fall into trouble through this medium of expression are:

(1) Murmuring: This is usually against God. The children of Israel were much given to this . . . "I don't know why God brought us out here in the wilderness . . . we are all going to die . . . we were better off back in Egypt, anyhow." Perhaps *this* response is more familiar to present-day ears: "I don't know why God treats me like this . . . I pay my tithe . . . I go to church every Sunday . . ."

(2) Criticizing: This is directed against our fellow believers . . . "they sing too long . . they sing too loud . . . why did they turn up the air-conditioning . . . purple shirts aren't for church . . ."

(3) Complaining: Here we have the second cousin

of the critical spirit. It is not hard to develop a complaining spirit once we entertain the critical. Have you ever gone out one day feeling that all was well with the world and then met up with a chronic complainer? It only took a short while for you to begin to wonder how you could possibly have imagined anything was right.

Notice, there are no rules that govern the spirit that projects itself in murmuring . . . criticizing . . . complaining.

A second phrase from Psalm 19:14 reads: ". . . the meditations of my heart." This is where the "words of my mouth" are born and nurtured. Meditation is a beautiful word. It literally means to "cast up again". It is the same word used in speaking of a cow chewing her cud. It pictures having swallowed something, bringing it back up, and enjoying it all over again. We hear some new truth in a meeting. Driving home we bring it to mind again. It is there when we awaken the next morning. But there is a reverse cycle to the advantage of reliving a new truth. There is that pretty girl in front of me . . . I push her image down into the recess of my inner thoughts . . . and before I know it, up it comes again. Those things I push down have a way of bubbling up and running around in my head. This is the area of no rules. This is where God wants to come in and do a thorough cleaning job. Mark 7:21-23 tells us: "Out of the heart proceedeth . . . evil thoughts . . . covetousness . . . deceit . . . pride."

WARFARE AND WEAPONS

Do you realize that we are all actively engaged in

actual spiritual warfare? Are you aware of the enemies . . . of the provisions made for us as we wage this battle? Two portions of Scripture will help us here:

II Corinthians 10:3-6 puts it this way: "For though we walk in the flesh (that is, the earthly, physical body) we do not war after the flesh. For the weapons of our warfare are not carnal, but mighty through God to the pulling down of strongholds: (casting down of the thoughts and the intents of the heart . . . all of these imaginations *can* be brought under control). Casting down imaginations, and every high thing that exalteth itself against the knowledge of God, and bringing in captivity every thought to the obedience (or, so that you will hear under Christ . . . that Christ will rule in your mental faculties) of Christ; and having in a readiness to revenge all disobedience."

When will God be able to deal with those persons and circumstances which you feel are causing your troubles? When God has been able to deal with the meditations of your heart . . . when the words of your mouth are the expressions of that cleansed heart . . . that is when God can begin to deal with that pastor . . . that parent . . . that husband or wife who seems to be your roadblock. It has blessed me to learn that as soon as I can get God to take care of ME, then He can change circumstances and persons where necessary.

II Timothy 2:24-26 sheds light on this warfare, too: "And the servant of the Lord must not strive: (with the woman who works next to me, even if she drains the coffee pot and doesn't put on any more; and takes my parking place when she comes to work in the morning) but be gentle unto all men, apt to teach, patient, in meekness, instructing those that oppose themselves; if God peradventure will give them repentance to the acknowledging of the truth: And that they may recover themselves out of the snare of the devil, who are taken captive by him at his will (this is what may be called a spiritual prisoner of war)."

Can you see that there are spiritual prisoners of war . . . captives, casualties and fatalities? A spiritual prisoner of war is one whose condition of heart keeps him in bondage. He may talk joy . . . shout louder and study more than anyone else . . . and yet be in captivity to an inward spirit which prevents true joy and freedom. The person who refuses to permit God to deal with him in the realm where there are no rules, never knows release from the covetous thing that makes him want to steal . . . never experiences freedom from the lustful eye that makes "thou shalt not commit adultery" a barrier to true fulfillment of our God-given natures.

I have found as I have experienced a measure of freedom in this spirit of obedience that I do not speak as loosely as before. The more I come under this spirit, the less I have to say. There is no longer any need to keep up with the "sea lawyers" . . . no need to spin tales . . . "I caught a fish fourteen pounds . . ." All need for boasting and pretense disappears!

How do we secure freedom as a spiritual prisoner of war? Certainly not by human will power. Life was never designed for us to live it by that method. If we try it, God will take us through the School of Failure. As we look to Him from our position of defeat, we can hear Him say, "If you will come My way, you will find the answer. My way has built into it the ability you need — that ability of the Spirit of God." Did you realize that Christianity is the only way of life that tells you what to do and then gives you the ability to do it?

ENCOUNTER AND ENABLEMENT

In order to more closely examine the source of power which God has provided, we read Romans 8:9-15.

(9) "But ye are not in the flesh, but in the Spirit, if so be that the Spirit of God dwell in you. (Next Paul makes a parenthetical statement which could have been put in a bracket); *Now if any man have not the Spirit of Christ, he is none of his.*

(10) "And if Christ be in you, the body is dead because of sin; but the Spirit is life because of righteousness.

(11) "But if the Spirit of him that raised up Jesus from the dead dwell in you, he that raised up Christ from the dead, shall also quicken your mortal bodies by the Spirit that dwelleth in you.

(12) "Therefore, brethren, we are debtors, not to the flesh, to live after the flesh.

(13) "For if ye live after the flesh, ye shall die; but if you through the Spirit do mortify the deeds of the body, ye shall live.

(14) "For as many as are led by the Spirit of God, they are the sons of God.

(15) "For as ye have not received the spirit of bondage again to fear; but ye have received the Spirit of adoption, whereby we cry, Abba, Father."

While reading a book, *The Spirit of Christ,* by Andrew Murray, a beautiful distinction in the ministry of the Holy Spirit was made alive to me. A careful study of the portion of Scripture above reveals a difference in the office work of the Spirit — it is the same Spirit, but the Spirit of Christ and the Spirit of God differ in administration. We know that God does not waste words or use the wrong word in the wrong place, so we can proceed on that certainty.

When we meet Jesus Christ in our initial encounter, we meet Him (1) as the Lamb of God. "Behold the Lamb of God which comes to take away the sin of the world" (John 2:29). (2) as Baptizer in the Holy Spirit. ". . . the same is he which baptizeth with the Holy Ghost" (John 1:33).

As we meet Jesus as the Lamb of God and are regenerated, the Holy Spirit comes to do a work *in* my life. I take on the nature of Christ — He imparts to me a new nature. In that nature comes a tremendous cry in my spirit that says, "Oh God, I want to do your will." Now I find I have the desire to do the will of God, but how to secure the ability to do it, eludes me.

Consider Jesus at the age of twelve. He is in the temple talking to the wise men of His day. When His mother chides Him for lingering in the temple instead of returning to Nazareth with the family, He says, "Mother, don't you understand? There is something working in Me that says I must be about My Father's business."

After many years of silence Jesus comes to the River Jordan to be baptized by John the Baptist. Jesus is about to be launched out into the work of obedience, into the fulfillment of His ministry. As

Jesus stands in the Jordan, God spoke to John and said, "The one on whom you see the Spirit of God descending . . ." Do you understand that the Spirit of Christ stood in the water — that is the *nature* of Christ. The Spirit of God comes down upon Him. As Jesus steps out of the water, He says: "The Spirit of the Lord is upon me . . . to release the captive . . . to open blind eyes . . . to heal the sick . . ."

The Spirit of Christ is that which gives you life. It brings with it the desire that God has provided for us to do His will (Philippians 1:19). Then the Spirit of God comes upon the believer and there is an *enabling* to do that will of God which has been birthed within.

As I looked at the life of the Apostle Paul, I asked, "God, what did that man have that enabled him to be stoned, thrown out of the city, and then he could get up — bruised and beaten — and go right back into the same situation? He had not only a desire to do Your will, but he also had the ability to do it!" Later I discovered that not only had God given Paul the power to do this, but God has made it available to all of us. Acts 1:8 tells us, "And you shall be witnesses unto me, *after that the power of the Holy Spirit comes upon you.*"

Our entrance into the Kingdom and our enabling to make progress in the life of the Kingdom are both the work of the Spirit. The Spirit of Christ brings us our new nature and then the Spirit of God comes upon us in order to energize that desire which is crying out to do God's will. It lifts the desire into the realm of actuating, performing, accomplishing. The emphasis is no longer only on wanting to do His will, but it is on doing it. Many people honestly want to do God's will but lack the power.

In Paul's words of instruction to one of the early churches regarding this power God has provided (I Corinthians 14:2 and 4), we find confirmation of this enabling principle. Please try to understand that the baptism in the Holy Spirit was not then — and is not now — primarily a "power tool". This priceless gift is not to be considered only as giving the ability to "perform signs and wonders". It does include such ability — but there is more — much more! *The baptism in the Holy Spirit is that anointing which grants us the ability to do the will of God. It is given to enable us to meet the demands of the Father!*

My Heavenly Father says to me, "Go to New Zealand and speak."

My reply to that command is, "God, I can't go to New Zealand and speak. I don't know what to say to them."

His assurance comes, "I will be with you. My Spirit shall be upon you and I will anoint you to do what I have asked you to do."

Listen again to Paul as he tells of God's provision for securing this power (verse 2): "For he that speaketh in an unknown tongue speaketh not unto men, but unto God: for no man understandeth him: howbeit in the spirit he speaketh mysteries." Here is prayer going up from within the child of God in "other tongues". It is reaching the very throne of God. It is prayer that I would never dare pray if I were praying in my own tongue. I may be saying, "God, see this rebel mouth that will not come under submission? Lord, do something about it!" Chances are I would never be bold enough to ask this of my own volition.

Again (verse 4): "He that speaketh in an unknown

tongue edifieth himself . . ." Is it selfish to be "built up"? Of course not. It is necessary. Is it possible to be called upon to help others and have so many problems yourself that you cannot respond? Learning to pray in the Spirit enables me to rise up and do that which God has spoken to me. Why was Jesus baptized in the Spirit of God? His answer was: "The Spirit of the Lord is upon me to release the captives . . . open blind eyes . . ." What is involved is the anointing — that ability to do what God commands.

TWELVE STEPS ALONG THE WAY

Before we bring into focus the enablements God has provided, notice that He never asks anything of us for which He has not first given us an anointing. Read carefully the one phrase that accompanies the miraculous exploits of these giants of the faith. "But the Spirit of God came on Gideon . . . the Spirit of God came on Abraham . . . the Spirit of God came on Samson . . . the Spirit of God came on Paul . . . the Spirit of God came on Peter . . ." That same Spirit is poured out in every generation to meet the Father's demands.

1. Our initial experience we shall call regeneration . . salvation . . . being born again. We meet the Lamb of God, get our house cleaned . . . receive a new nature, which is called the Spirit of Christ — the nature of Jesus. (John 1:29)

2. According to the New Testament, baptism in water should follow — for the release of the old man and the bringing up of the new man. (Acts 2:38)

3. We receive the baptism in the Holy Spirit — that is the Spirit of God, which affords, if properly used

and understood, the ability to do the will of God. We move from the realm of "I wish I could" to find God has granted us the 'I can". (Acts 2:38)

4. Understand and appropriate your ability to worship and praise in other tongues. Keep your well open and flowing. The Spirit of God is given to build us up. (I Corinthians 14:2,4)

5. Recognize that obedience, like submission, is a discipline. It is something we learn. It does not come naturally. (Hebrews 5:8)

6. Take it one day at a time. Never come to the place where you feel you can say, "Glory to God. Look at this obedient servant!" This is asking for trouble! (Luke 9:23)

7. Listen carefully to all instructions. Check them out with your three guides: The Word of God, the Spirit, and the authority over you. Ask for a "repeat" if you feel it is necessary. God will always honor that request. (Isaiah 50:4)

8. Once you have received your instructions, obey them to the best of your ability. Remember, failure is part of the lesson. At times we may be given an assignment that staggers us and as we move out to obey, we find it to be more than we can handle. This is God's opportunity to come and instruct us with some "on the job training". Never hesitate to call upon Him when you hit a snag. That is what He is waiting for – your plea for His help. (Acts 26:19)

9. If you sense even the slightest inward resistance, take careful pains to make certain that you deal with it and that it breaks. Once you meet that inward resistance that rises against the will of God, it is your responsibility to recognize it and deal with it until you experience peace. (Romans 6:17)

10. Be careful of hasty, urgent, demanding voices. Anything that is of this nature, is suspect. I have found that God always begins soon enough to get me to the right place at the right time. Every time I have been on a crash program for Jesus, it crashed! Guard against over-eagerness to obey and cultivate the spirit of obedience. (Colossians 3:15)

11. Remember that it is not past experience that counts — it is present attitude. God never permits assumption of past performance to be a platform for continuing anointing. When He checks for "grapes", He will not be satisfied with "leaves". (Romans 7:4)

12. Examine your own life pattern to find out whether your progress is registered as a series of continual "breakings", or whether you have been broken by God and are walking in humility and obedience — developing a hearing ear and responsive spirit. (Psalm 40:6)

God never ordained or intended that the Christian life be one constant series of breakings and crises. He has arranged these twelve steps that we might walk forward with confidence into the normal growth pattern He has ordained. As we walk with Him in humbleness and openness — as we become increasingly sensitive, not only to sin but to any tinge of rebellion — we stabilize our lives and enjoy the even keel of sailing out into the open waters of fellowship. And fellowship with God and with each other is that for which we were created!

When we are freed from the Great Transgression, we find ourselves enjoying and exemplifying the Nature and Spirit of Obedience. The Spirit of obedience, working within the deep of our human spirit, produces joy and fruitfulness in daily Christian

OTHER BOOKS BY BOB MUMFORD

Take Another Look At Guidance

15 Steps Out

Christ in Session: Introduction
    To the Body of Christ

Living Happily Ever After

*These books and other interesting subjects available
on Audio-Cassette from:*
> *P.O. Box 22341*
> *Ft. Lauderdale, Florida 33315*